acts:

working together in christ's mission

J. Estill Jones

CONVENTION PRESS
A CHURCH SERVICES AND MATERIALS DIVISION PRODUCT

Contents

1 Together at Jerusalem...**6**

2 Lessons in Problem Solving: *Jerusalem*...**19**

3 The Scattered Church: *Jerusalem to Samaria and Caesarea*...**32**

4 The Mission of Peter: *Judea and Caesarea*...**43**

5 The Developing Crisis: *Damascus, Antioch, and Beyond* ...**54**

6 Freedom at Jerusalem...**70**

7 A Needy World: *Macedonia*...**83**

8 Challenging Cities: *Athens and Corinth*...**96**

9 A Mission Center: *Ephesus*...**110**

10 Christ's Unfettered Witness: *Jerusalem to Rome*....**125**

Personal Learning Activities...**140**

© Copyright 1974 • Convention Press
Church Services and Materials Division
Allen B. Comish, *Director*
Nashville, Tennessee
All rights reserved

5132-15

Art credits: John Teh, Haskell Richardson
Photo credits: Foreign Mission Board,
Division of Visual Education

This book is the text for course 3215
of the New Church Study Course

Dewey Decimal classification number: 226.6
Printed in the United States of America

Preface

Acts can be read and understood in a variety of ways. For example, it can be read as a kind of third person diary, giving the chronicle of the gospel's geographical advance. For that kind of reading, maps are important. The journeys of the early Christian missioners are traced out; pleasure is taken in the gospel's forward movement. The experience is interesting, and tends to confirm the reader's Christian faith.

Another way of reading and understanding Acts builds on the idea of the gospel's spread. In addition to the maps, this way of reading the book requires empathy of the reader. That is, he must enter into the inner sweep of the Acts events. He is sensitive to the influences and backgrounds which create differing points of view within the Christian fellowship. Emotions are felt; the tension of conflict is real. Such a reading partakes of life as we know it.

In this way of reading, the Holy Spirit's leadership in Acts is seen in three dimensions: movement in time, in place, and in the persons involved. There is a depth of reality that corresponds with the reader's own experience.

Our writer has worked to achieve the effect of both ways of reading and understanding Acts. We see the physical advance of the gospel, but we see more. We are permitted an in-depth view of the friction that sometimes develops in close interpersonal relationships. We see the clashing of opposing understandings of gospel truth. We see motives—both good and bad—as they operate in person's lives. In it all, we see God at work through his Spirit, helping men grasp the deeper gospel truths and all that those truths imply.

Dr. Estill Jones has brought to the writing of these pages a background of training and experience that fits him for this demanding task. The first years of his ministry were spent as a teacher of young preachers at The Southern Baptist Theological Seminary in Louisville, Kentucky. In those years, our writer taught the Greek language and New Testament interpretation. Beginning in 1959 Dr. Jones served three years as the pastor of the First Baptist Church, Chatsworth, Georgia. An eleven-year pastorate at Thomson, Georgia's First Baptist Church followed. Shortly after accepting this writing assignment, he moved from Thomson to the Dogwood Hills Baptist Church of East Point, Georgia—a suburb of Atlanta. He serves that church now. Dr. Jones' rich background of experience, plus his interpretation skills, serves us all in our 1975 January Bible Study textbook.

As you read these pages, you will find yourself and your own fellow church members. You will recognize the similarity between problems existing in the first-century church and your own. We hope that you will read with a mounting confidence in God's power to direct, through his Spirit, church members and churches as they seek to work together in Christ's mission.

Ralph L. Murray

The Editor
Nashville, Tennessee

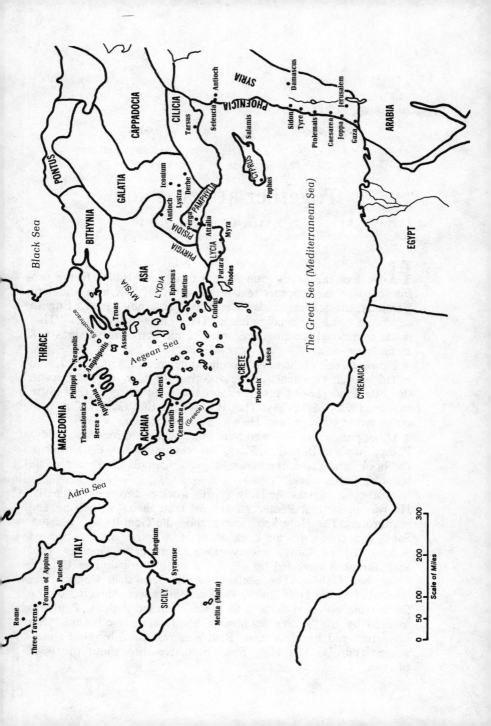

Together at Jerusalem

Acts 1:1 to 4:31

How does the heading on Acts read in your Bible? In the version used as the Scripture text for this study (American Standard Version), the heading reads "The Acts." You may have an English version in which the heading reads "The Acts of the Apostles." That is the traditional heading, and most of the Scripture versions will carry that reading.

However, one of the most prominent persons in Acts is Paul, who called himself "the least of the apostles" (1 Cor. 15:9). Beyond that, Paul interpreted his Christian life in terms of a God-given mission (Acts 26:16-23). That is, Paul felt that God was at work in the world through him. He was a tool God used.

Other persons in Acts who were not apostles are recalled readily: Philip, Stephen, Barnabas, Silas, Timothy, and—yes, the author of the book himself—Luke. They, also, were tools God used to do his work in the world.

Moreover, in Acts the Holy Spirit's work is drawn quite clearly. He was present at Pentecost. He used Stephen's witnessing and martyrdom. The Holy Spirit came upon the Gentiles at Caesarea. Saul's conversion was the work of the Holy Spirit. Antioch became a center of the Spirit's mighty moving among the Gentiles. Paul and Barnabas were led by the Spirit in their mission to Cyprus, Syria, and Galatia. The decision of the Jerusalem Council was attributed to the Holy Spirit. Paul and Silas were directed by the Spirit from northern Galatia to Macedonia and Achaia. Paul was assured by the Spirit's leading in his Jerusalem offering. After his arrest and imprisonment, Paul was reassured by God's messenger (angel). The Holy Spirit is active throughout the book of Acts.

Whose acts do we study, then? Whatever else we may say, this must be said: These are God's acts. God, who acted through Abraham, Moses, and the prophets; God, who acted in Christ—this is the God who, by the power of his Spirit and the willingness of his people, acts. The book of Acts is the record of God's acts. God was acting through his people, who by working together, were fulfilling Christ's mission. It is not different today.

1. Understanding the Book of Acts (1:1-11)

Prologue (1:1-5)
The introductory verses to the book of Acts relate the gospel proclaimed by Jesus in word and deed to the church's continuing work. Jesus' followers speak and act, but they major on *his* lines and *his* actions. His Spirit serves as director. They trust in Jesus' promise: "Ye shall be baptized in the Holy Spirit" (1:5). The author connects the Gospel of Luke to the book of Acts: "The former treatise I made, O Theophilus, concerning all that Jesus began both to do and to teach" (Acts 1:1). Luke was devoted to "those matters which have been fulfilled among us" (1:1). Acts describes the actions of those who witnessed that fulfillment.

Theophilus' identity is not revealed. Indeed, the name of Luke himself appears in neither volume. Perhaps Theophilus was the patron who encouraged the writing. Tradition supposes as much. His name serves to relate the Gospel to the Acts. This dedication is the obvious relationship, but it is confirmed by Acts' consistency to the Gospel in style and content.

The book of Acts must be understood against the background of Jesus' ministry. The book's purpose is suggested in these first brief paragraphs. Since the kingdom of God was a favorite theme in Jesus' ministry, the prologue includes this theme in its summary of the days after the resurrection: "Speaking the things concerning the kingdom of God" (v. 3).

A Significant Question (1:6-8)
Perhaps Jesus' emphasis on the kingdom led the apostles to ask him the question, "Lord, dost thou at this time restore the kingdom to Israel?" (v. 6). Their question was loaded, and reflected their nationalistic hopes. They do not appear to have shared Jesus' understanding of a spiritual kingdom, but expressed the old messianic hope of a new Davidic kingdom. Jesus' use of the term "kingdom" referred to God's sovereignty, God's realm. It

was limited by neither geographical nor political boundaries. The disciples had indicated similar misunderstanding before Jesus' death. What beyond the resurrection could shake them loose from the popular Jewish hope?

The Lord's reply was gentle—an appeal to faith in the Father (v. 7). The earlier promise of the Holy Spirit was repeated. His power would enable them to expand their vision, to deepen their insight, to break the chains of national prejudice, and to offer freely to all men the kingdom of God (v. 8).

A popular outline of the book of Acts traces the movement of the gospel from Jerusalem to Judea; then to Samaria, and, finally, to the uttermost parts of the earth. This view of Acts is valid. However, another movement, equally important, occurs in Acts. That is Christianity's movement from a narrow Hebrew cell to persons of Greek and other Gentile origins. In this development all people were offered citizenship in the kingdom of God. Acts does not tell, as a matter of fact, all the means by which the gospel reached the "uttermost parts." The arrival of the apostle Paul in Rome is described, but he is welcomed by Christians already there.

Dr. Frank Stagg has made an excellent case for the adverb "unhinderedly." [1] This is the last word in the Greek text of Acts. It may well describe the freedom finally attained by the gospel, which is suggested at the outset of the book (v. 8). So understood, Acts is the story of the struggle for an unhindered gospel. All barriers became as nothing before the power of the Holy Spirit. The kingdom of God became real in the lives of all kinds of men and women. The emphasis is on the restoration of *Israel* to the kingdom, not the *kingdom* to Israel! That Jesus and his followers talked about the kingdom (vv. 6-8) before the work in Christ's mission began is significant.

The same careful techniques used in volume 1 (Luke 1:1-4) are evident in volume 2 (Acts 1:1-5). These techniques include the gathering of information, and its orderly development. Accurate dating for the book is difficult. A generally acceptable date for the Gospel is after the destruction of Jerusalem in A.D. 70, and perhaps would push the book of Acts into the decade of the eighties. By this time, Jewish Christianity would have become largely historical. The narrative would be of primary interest to the Gentile Christians who, like Theophilus, desired reassurance as to the beginnings.

The identity of Luke, the beloved physician (Col. 4:14), as author is the reflection of an old tradition. Of interest with respect to the authorship is the introduction of a first person pronoun into the narrative of Acts 16:10. When Paul saw the Macedonian vision in Troas, immediately *"we* sought to go forth into Macedonia." This suggests that the author may have joined the party in that vicinity. Later (16:19), the "we" section ceases, only to be resumed in 20:6. The book generally has been accepted by the church as an accurate account of its earliest years. The author was inspired by the power of the Holy Spirit to record the events.

2. The Church Gathered (1:12-26)

Jesus' abrupt departure might well have torn the disciples apart. They had recovered somewhat from their grief at his death. They had been with him for forty days. Their hopes, rekindled by his presence, were now dashed by his departure. They were, however, together. In fact, the followers of Jesus were distinguished by their togetherness. The words used to describe their fellowship are varied: "With one accord" (v. 14), "the midst of the brethren" (v. 15), "together" (v. 15), "all together" (2:1). The most significant word—*koinonia*—appears later, in 2:44. That word describes a mutuality in their relationship, which should be the goal of every church fellowship. No one of the group claimed his own rights or possessions—they had all things in common. Although some will charge these early Christians were more idealistic than realistic, the facts of their love for one another and their spiritual power are quite clear.

What should they do together? When Jesus had faced a crisis, he prayed—and he had encouraged them to pray. So they prayed "with one accord" (1:14). Only one of the original twelve apostles had been lost from the fellowship. Judas' treason and death must have shaken Simon Peter especially. He himself had come close to desertion. It was not a pretty picture. The author described how the church filled the leadership vacancy left by Judas' tragic end (1:16-26).

The new member of the twelve was required to be a witness to the resurrection. This was primary, but he also must have been with them from Jesus' baptism through his ascension. Nothing further is known of Matthias (who was chosen), but then Acts has nothing to say about most of the twelve. They were in fellow-

ship—a major feat. They completed their organization after prayer
—and waited for God's power to come. Was God's power available for his church?

3. The Coming of the Holy Spirit (2:1-47)

The Feast of Pentecost was a significant Jewish observance. In
practice it was an agricultural celebration, marking the fiftieth day
after the offering of the sheaf of the first-ripe barley. This offering
was a part of the Feast of Unleavened Bread. Pentecost, the Feast
of Weeks,[2] was so named because it was scheduled fifty days, or
seven weeks, after Passover. Jewish men were expected to be at
this feast, as well as at Passover and Tabernacles. Jews came to
Jerusalem from all over the world for the feast. The particular
Passover in that year's festive calendar had witnessed the crucifixion of Jesus. His friends, however, had already found strength
in his resurrection and in their togetherness.

The Event (2:1-8)
The Spirit's coming cannot be separated from his effect on those
who experienced and witnessed his presence. Luke is even more
brief in detail here than in the description of the crucifixion and
the resurrection. The experience was fundamentally spiritual in
nature.

There was "a sound as of the rushing of a mighty wind" (v. 2),
and the house was filled with it. The word which Luke used can
be translated either *spirit* or *wind*. The vision of the "tongues . . .
as of fire" (v. 3) was shared by the group. Their own tongues
were loosed by the Spirit. The Spirit filled these early witnesses and
gave them something to say.

The Effect (2:9-11)
The effect of Pentecost closely relates to the event. There were
Jews present from everywhere. These Jews usually felt ill at ease because of their inability to understand and use the Hebrew tongue.
Hearing the commotion, many of these came *together* and listened
to men speak in their own language of the mighty works of God.
They heard and understood. The Tower of Babel experiment ended
in a confusion of tongues (Gen. 11:1-9) and separateness. Pentecost provided understanding and togetherness.

The Explanation (2:12-38)
As is frequently true, the mob sought a physical explanation for
this spiritual event: "They are filled with new wine" (2:13). The
charge called for an explanation; Peter's sermon was the result.

It was much too early in the day for drunkenness (Peter said), but never too early for the Spirit to work. The explanation related Pentecost to the prophecy of Joel (2:28-32). Then Peter told of Jesus' life and death. The forty days with Jesus after the resurrection had not been in vain. Peter's references to the Psalms are similar to Jesus' interpretation of them. The early church believed that the prophecies of the Old Testament were fulfilled in the ministry of Jesus, and in the Spirit's indwelling their midst.

The sermons of Acts accord perfectly with that which we know about the early Christians' beliefs. Luke apparently enjoyed access to the principals in the story, and to others who witnessed the events. For the most part the sermons contain the core of the gospel. They are referred to as the *kerygma,* about which C. H. Dodd has written:

> In its most summary form the *kerygma* consists of the announcement of certain historical events in a setting which displays the significance of those events. The events in question are those of the appearance of Jesus in history—His ministry, sufferings and death and His subsequent manifestation of Himself to His followers as risen from the dead and invested with the glory of another world—and the emergence of the Church as a society distinguished by the power and activity of the Holy Spirit, and looking forward to the return of its Lord as Judge and Saviour of the world.[3]

This statement provides a good summary of the gospel as preached in the early church. All these events were a part of God's redemptive purpose.

The challenge to the multitude, "Let all the house of Israel therefore know . . ." (2:36), pricked their conscience ("cut to the heart" [v. 37, NEB][4]). When Peter charged the "house of Israel" with the crucifixion of their long-awaited Messiah, they both heard and understood. God had granted Christ lordship, even as he had attested his messiahship. The intervention of the crucifixion could not prevent God's purpose. The final victory belongs to God.

Peter did not deal profoundly with theological problems. He fitted his good news to his hearers. His clear invitation has become classic, and yet it is closely related to the consistent cry of John the Baptist, "Repent ye" (Matt. 3:2). The ancient prophets called on Israel to "turn" (Isa. 31:6; Joel 2:12-13). Repentance picks up that cry: "Turn from your rejection of Jesus; turn to

God." Perhaps some of these had heard reports of John's witness and baptism. Had he not spoken of just such an event? (See Luke 3:16.)

Everyone was included in the invitation, although many, having come to Jerusalem for the first time, had had nothing to do with Jesus' death. Everyone was to repent; everyone was to subject himself to the cleansing judgment of God. This was symbolized in the Christian rite of baptism, and everyone was to be baptized. Later, more profound explanations of baptism would be made (Rom. 6:1-11), but here it simply follows repentance. The promise of forgiveness is consistent with God's mercy.

Verse 38 is cited often as proof that baptism is essential to salvation. That interpretation rests on the proof text method of Bible interpretation. One rule for the interpretation of any Bible verse is that the explanation be true to the clear teachings found elsewhere in the New Testament. The uniform teaching of the New Testament is that faith in Christ and his atoning work is the basis of salvation. (See Gal. 3:13-14; Eph. 2:8-10; 1 Pet. 2:22-25; John 3:36.) God does not use baptism to produce salvation.

The key word *(eis)* in Acts 2:38 is translated variously: "unto" (ASV); "for" (KJV, RSV, NEB); "so that" (TEV).[5] The translation of *eis* by any of the words cited seems to suggest that salvation is the result of faith in Christ and baptism. Those who teach baptism as a vital part of salvation take the verse that way. However, the Greek word *eis,* used with the accusative case, can be translated in a causal sense. That is, baptism can be the result of faith in Christ, not the partial means of salvation. In a discussion of this passage, Dr. Frank Stagg presents a translation in keeping with the plain teaching of the New Testament, and faithful to the Greek construction: " 'Repent, and let each of you be baptized in the name of Jesus Christ *on the basis of* (author's italics) the forgiveness of your sins, and you shall receive the free gift of the Holy Spirit.' "[6]

The Extension (2:39-47)

The promise of the Holy Spirit belongs to the repentant, for God calls such people to himself, even those "that are afar off" (v. 39). Thus the good news of God in Christ extended to a great group of non-Palestinian Jews. Three thousand who believed were baptized, and they joined the fellowship in Jerusalem. Some day, however, they would return to Parthia, Mesopotamia, Egypt, and Rome, and become witnesses there to these events.

Pentecost is a dramatic scene in this book of Acts. The event was the filling of these early witnesses with the Holy Spirit. The effect was massive understanding: "We hear them speaking in our tongues the mighty works of God" (2:11). The explanation was a gospel sermon. The extension of the gospel seemed assured. This was Pentecost!

The believers were together. The apostles were teaching. The fellowship was attractive. They ate and prayed together. They went to the Temple daily, together. They had a good reputation in Jerusalem. "And the Lord added to them day by day those that were saved" (2:47). What could you expect from a fellowship like that? You might expect some opposition from those who opposed Jesus. And you might expect a miracle.

4. The Healing of the Lame Man (3:1-10)

Together at the Temple (3:1-5)
The events portrayed in Acts were clearly selected from many that might have been included. This particular event merited treatment. The church had not yet broken with the Temple. Much of Jesus' ministry in Jerusalem had been in the vicinity of the Temple; thus his followers found it a choice place to gather. Certain hours were regarded as preferable for prayer. Peter and John chose an afternoon hour. The Temple, like the modern church, was not only a good place for prayer, but also for alms asking and almsgiving.

What an enviable spot for the lame beggar—at the door of the Temple! This says something about people who came to the Jewish Temple. The lame man expected worshipers to be a soft touch; he came to the place where help could be expected. Since begging was an honorable occupation for a lame man, he took his post daily.

Peter and John, influential leaders of the Christian church, were likely prospects. He asked them for alms. They gave more than he asked; they gave what they had. The translation of verse 6 in *The New English Bible* is especially clear: "What I have I give." What would a modern worshiper do? Would he send the beggar to the city or county authorities? Would he seek to ignore his cries? Would he hurry into the prayer service? Peter stopped and stared: "Look on us" (v. 4). Now the expectation of the lame man was kindled. Peter and John sensed the man's deeper need; they knew their own resources. They believed that God could meet the man's every need. Perhaps someone else could give the man silver or gold; they could give him God's healing gift.

The Event (3:6-8)

All this leads up to the event: the man's healing. The healing was God's act, and the appeal for it was made by God's people in the name of Jesus Christ (v. 6). Pronouncing the name of Jesus was not a magical incantation, but a prayer. Jesus had encouraged his followers to ask "in my name" (John 14:13-14). (The name of a man was frequently an indication of his character. Deity's name was sacred and reserved for prayerful petitions. The book of Acts reflects and respects this significance. Little wonder that disrespect for God's name is described as profanity—profaning the name of deity.)

The word was followed by the miracle. A word alone is meaningless, for the word must become flesh to be heard. Peter took the man's hand—was it dirty? or deformed?—and lifted him to his feet. (This disciple of Jesus was like neither the priest nor the Levite who passed by on the other side [see Luke 10:30-32]. He involved himself with the lame man.) New strength came into the man's ankles; new life came into the man's bones.

The Effect (3:9-11)

The immediate effect was the crowd's amazement. The healed man entered the Temple with Peter and John—and would not let them out of his sight. Peter and John had given what they had ("What I have I give!"), and the healed man followed their example: He walked and leaped and praised God (v. 8). "The people saw him" (v. 9). A genuine healing, whether physical or spiritual, is exciting to the popular mind. It always draws a crowd together. How many of them had passed the man by, or dropped a mite into his hand? How many of them had wondered why he was lame?

The Explanation (3:12-26)

Peter's explanation followed in the form of a sermon. How could Peter resist explaining the deed? The outline of the sermon is similar to others—then and now:

God continues active (vv. 12-15)—
  despite your rejection of Jesus;
  despite crucifixion;
  as evidenced by the resurrection.
This man has believed in Jesus (v. 16)—
  you know this man;
  he has been healed.
You too may know God's blessing (vv. 17-26)—
  repent and be forgiven;
  accept Jesus as the Promised One;
  enjoy all the blessings of God.

The sermon's illustration was quite clear: the lame man's healing. The hope Jesus fulfilled had been expected through well-nigh endless generations—Moses, and all the prophets, beginning with Samuel, and "them that followed after" (3:24). It extended back to Abraham and God's promise to him. It would find its ultimate fulfillment in the "restoration of all things" (3:21) when the Lord returns.

Church Growth (4:1-4)

The gathering of the crowd provoked the authorities. As a result, Peter and John were arrested. Nevertheless, since the deed had been done, and the word had been heard, church growth was inevitable. Many heard and believed, and the congregation numbered about five thousand.

The event was the healing of the lame man; the effect was immediate popularity for Peter and John; the explanation was a gospel sermon; the extension of the gospel was to two thousand more believers. They and the apostles were together at Jerusalem.

5. Trial and Release (4:5-20,23,31)

A Meeting of the Sanhedrin (4:5-7)

The forces opposed to the Christian church were also together at Jerusalem. The names of the leading persons are familiar: Annas, a former high priest, and Caiaphas, who now held that office (John 18:24). The high priesthood by this time had become a political plum, awarded to the highest bidder by the Roman government. The only real requirement appears to have been that it remain in the family. In the time of Jesus, Caiaphas was high priest; Annas, his father-in-law, was head of the family. Although John and Alexander (4:6) are not so familiar to the modern reader, they may have been well known to those about whom Luke wrote. The extension of the gospel is noted a bit later: "A great company of the priests were obedient to the faith" (6:7). Perhaps Luke was anticipating that development here. Of interest is the acquaintance between the other disciple of John 18:15 and the high priest.

The Sanhedrin met in desperation. Having rid themselves of Jesus, they were not about to be overwhelmed by his followers. The court of inquiry centered on the miraculous healing. They could argue about the sermon, but that the man had been healed was hardly subject to question. Their inquiry was an exercise in futility: "In what name have ye done this?" (4:7).

A Gospel Sermon (4:8-12)

The Sanhedrin's question prompted a brief gospel sermon. It set forth the idea that Jesus' crucifixion was followed by his resurrection; that the lame man's healing was done in the power of Jesus' name. Further, Peter contended that these developments were the fulfillment of prophecy; that in Jesus the way of salvation could be found. Peter is described as "filled with the Holy Spirit" (v. 8). He had the boldness of the Spirit for this testimony. Had not Jesus promised as much? (See Matt. 10:19-20.)

The power residing in Jesus' name is a frequent subject in these early chapters. Faith in the name of Jesus was one of the marks strongly characteristic of the primitive church. Jesus' name represented his essence: "Thou shalt call his name Jesus; for it is he that shall save his people from their sins" (Matt. 1:21). This salvation was reserved exclusively for those who believed in that name. Jesus' name remains the clearest expression of God's redemptive grace, for the name means "the Lord is salvation." Others before Jesus had borne that name, the Hebrew of which is Joshua. However, no other had been "the image of the invisible God" (Col. 1:15); no other had been the Word of God made flesh (John 1:14).

+ And what of the rejected stone (v. 11)? The rejected stone is a popular image in the New Testament. It may be traced to Psalm 118:22, which is a psalm of rejoicing in God's salvation. Was there a large stone in ancient Jerusalem, close by the building site of the Temple? The size of the stones which served as the Temple's foundation is remarkable. Was a large stone rejected, only to become the cornerstone later? Even now the world's largest stone is pointed out by the guides in the Middle East. It was quarried and partially moved, but still, after many centuries, it waits to be used in a worthy building project. This psalmist's stone caught the spiritual imagination of New Testament writers. Three of the Gospels include a reference to it by Jesus (Matt. 21:42; Mark 12:10; Luke 20:17). The letter to the Ephesians (2:20) uses the stone figure in reference to Jesus. So also does 1 Peter 2:7. The rejection motif is, of course, common to all Christian explanations of the cross. Men of Israel rejected Jesus, but God raised him. So God frustrated the evil purposes of men and fulfilled the ancient hopes of his own people.

The Helpless Sanhedrin (4:13-17)

The religious authorities faced a real dilemma. What *could* they do? How could they control these "ignorant men" (v. 13)? Although none had trained in the schools for rabbis, they were quite capable. After all, they had been with Jesus. His life and teachings were all they could talk about. The lame man stood there as a prime example of God's power; the rulers could not deny the miracle. Their utter frustration is amusing: How feebly the mighty struggled to control spiritual power! They did all they could: "Let us threaten them, that they speak henceforth to no man in this name" (v. 17).

Primary Loyalties (4:18-30)

The response of Peter and John was not disrespectful to the authorities. A noticeable restraint appears in the New Testament on this matter. Civil disobedience is not advocated in Acts. Dr. Stagg has underscored the protection which the Roman government offered the Christian church and its leaders.[7] Jewish leaders, however, proved especially troublesome. Even so, church leaders did not openly antagonize them. The church at Jerusalem, especially, does not appear to have ceased Temple worship through the years covered by the Acts account. That God's people obey him, however, and strive to bring society around to similar obedience, is a demand. When forced to choose, these Christians chose to obey God, not man (see 5:29). The apostles had seen and heard events which were undeniable. They might be silenced by death, but they could not deny what had happened.

Since no law had been violated, the apostles were released. Once again the church was together at Jerusalem. Now their witness included an account of the meeting with the Sanhedrin. In a sense, their way of life was vindicated by the inability of the ruling authorities to stop that witness. The unified praise recorded glorifies the power of God (vv. 24-30). Moreover, at the end of the prayer meeting God responded with new spiritual blessings.

A Surge of Power (4:31)

The precise nature of the Spirit's demonstration in the Christians' midst (v. 31) is hidden by the centuries, but the account indicates that a powerful visit of the Holy Spirit occurred. Some interpret this account as a repeat of the earlier coming, recorded in chapter 2. To suppose, however, that the Holy Spirit is confined to one such experience is to limit the power of God. Note that the second account does not include the speaking with tongues, a mark of the earlier experience. As they prayed together, the Holy Spirit came. Thus empowered, "They spoke the word of God with boldness" (v. 31).

6. Truth for Today

God's love extends to all men. From the beginning God has loved the world. God's people are to show and tell the world of that love. They may begin by sharing it with the stranger next door, or the foreigner down the street. The Christian's privilege is to help make God's love known to the world around.

God's Spirit dwells within his church. On occasion, God's Spirit may be found in powerful demonstrations of his presence. His Spirit may be experienced, also, in the warm togetherness which characterizes a true spiritual fellowship. The Holy Spirit draws the church together, and God's people are most effective in their ministry and witness when there is no question about their togetherness.

The church has surprising resources for ministry. God's power is beyond our imagination. He will help the churches in their work of ministry. The lame man asked for alms; he was granted healing. The modern beggar asks for money; he needs friendship, acceptance, counsel, and spiritual healing as well. The church offers all these.

Miracles help move the church forward. A part of our difficulty is our inability to communicate the miracles which happen. A young person who has "turned off" drugs and "turned on" to Jesus is a miracle. An influential adult who publicly confesses his Christian faith is a miracle. These miracles, repeated in the fellowship week by week, are quiet miracles that move the church forward.

Obedience to God is most important. More important than to succeed in business is to obey God's will. More important than to save one's life is to obey God's will. More important than to be popular or powerful or prosperous is to obey God's will.

---

[1] Frank Stagg, *The Book of Acts* (Nashville: Broadman Press, 1955), p. 1.

[2] Flavius Josephus, *The Life and Works of Flavius Josephus,* trans. by William Whiston (Philadelphia: The John C. Winston Company), p. 107: "When a week of weeks has passed over after this sacrifice (which weeks contain forty and nine days,), on the fiftieth day, which is Pentecost . . .." (See also Ex. 23:14-16; Lev. 23:15-16; Deut. 16:9-12; 2 Chron. 8:13.) In the early Christian centuries many observed Pentecost as the commemoration of the giving of the Law at Mt. Sinai, but there is no Old Testament evidence for this relationship.

[3] C. H. Dodd, *According to the Scriptures* (New York: Scribner's, 1953), pp. 11-12.

[4] From *The New English Bible.* © The Delegates of the Oxford University Press, and the Syndics of the Cambridge University Press, 1970. Reprinted by permission, as are all other quotations from this translation. Quotations from this version are indicated by the abbreviation NEB in parenthesis.

[5] From the *Today's English Version* of the New Testament. Copyright © American Bible Society, 1966, 1971. All succeeding quotations from this version are indicated by the abbreviation TEV in parenthesis.

[6] Stagg, *op. cit.,* pp. 62-63.

[7] *Ibid.,* p. 18.

Lessons in Problem Solving:
Jerusalem

Acts 4:32 to 6:7

To live is to grow. To grow is to relate to other persons. To relate is to solve problems. In a real sense living is problem solving. The church at Jerusalem grew rapidly. From the one hundred and twenty who shared in the selection of Matthias (1:15), to the three thousand added after Pentecost (2:41), "the number of the men came to be about five thousand" (4:4). Perhaps this number ought to be adjusted upward to include a number of women. We do not know exactly how the count was made.

The period of time involved in this rapid growth is not known either. The author may have compressed a series of events into what seems to be a short span of time. The description of the developing problems and their solutions is drawn masterfully. Since today's Christian fellowship faces similar problems, a natural question arises: Can the example of another church in another century, and in another context, help us?

1. Economic Insecurity (2:42-47; 4:32-37)

The setting of the action continues in Jerusalem. Two brief paragraphs hint at a problem and describe its solution (2:43-47; 4:32-37). Both follow an experience with the Holy Spirit. Omitting the details, Luke recorded only the solution to the growing problem. Jesus had recognized it: "The poor ye have always with you" (John 12:8).

The Jewish people look after their own, and always have. The bonds that tie the people together, though scattered over the world, are strong and durable. This fact has given rise historically to ghetto existence. It has also attracted the opposition of non-Jews.

In the New Testament period, regular collection and distribution of food was practiced. The wealthy contributed goods to the poor. The Christian fellowship also would minister to deeper needs.

The Problem (2:42-43)

Were the poor Christians in Jerusalem given a regular dole by their fellow Jews? If so, how did the opposition of the Jewish religious leaders tend to affect the practice? Would the wealthy Sadducees be sympathetic with the apostles and their followers? If a Christian should develop a personal need, how comfortably could he appeal to the Jerusalem Temple leaders for help?

Details are missing, but the men who followed Jesus had left their gainful occupations. At least four of them had been fishermen, but no longer. Another of the apostles had been a tax collector, perhaps even prosperous (see Luke 5:27-29); but no longer. Others of the twelve must have been in similar situations. Their incomes had been curtailed or terminated. In addition, a number of Galileans had followed Jesus to Jerusalem and had remained there after the resurrection. Thousands were gathering daily for "the apostles' teaching and fellowship, in the breaking of bread and the prayers" (2:42). Where was the bread to come from?

There was the problem. Translated into modern terms, it may have been the indifference of the "haves" to the needs of the "have-nots." It may have been the subtle opposition of prosperous church members to their church's social ministry. The refusal of a segment of a congregation today to support the budget could be a facet of this same problem. Is economic pressure ever applied toward the changing of the church's direction? More dangerous than opposition from outside is this inner division. Some churches have experienced such economic pressures. That is a problem.

The Solution (2:44-45)

The solution was simple: We will share. Already in basic agreement, they shared their physical assets as well. The word used to describe the practice is *koinos,* which may be translated "mutuality." They shared what they had. They renounced goods and rights. So long as there was food available to anyone, it was available to everyone. Thus the regular meals became spiritual experiences at which they enjoyed sharing. Later Paul was to rebuke Corinthian Christians for renouncing the principle: "Each of you is in such a hurry to eat his own, and while one goes hungry another has too much to drink. . . . Are you so contemptuous of the church of God that you shame its poorer members?" (1 Cor. 11:21-22, NEB).

When food gave out, as give out it did, what then? Those who had property sold it, brought the proceeds to the fellowship, and "laid them at the apostles' feet" (4:35). Thus the needs of the poor and rich alike were met by the application of the sharing principle: "What's mine is yours, and you can have it." That it was purely voluntary protects the early church from any contemporary charge of communism.

Was it good business to spend their capital in this manner? Perhaps use of their resources in this way was not wise. Some have supposed that the later famine conditions in the Jerusalem church might have been the result of their earlier charity. Their primary concern, however, was not building an endowment; it was building a fellowship—a mutuality of sharing—a *koinonia*. There was no longer need in the fellowship. The threat of economic insecurity had been overcome.

The Result (2:46-47; 4:36-37)

One of the side effects of a problem's solution is the enlistment of new leadership, perhaps the discovery of an able man. Nothing is really known of Barnabas prior to this experience. Although some scholars have supposed that he was one of the seventy sent out by Jesus (Luke 10:1-24), there is no New Testament evidence for that idea. That he should be introduced in this dramatic fashion is proper. Later he was to exercise strong leadership in the church. Barnabas was not his real name: it was Joseph. Frequently a surname simply included the father's name—as "Johnson" originally meant "John's son." Because of Joseph's generous deed, however, the apostles called him "Barnabas," which translated means "Son of Consolation" (4:36). He was a Levite, and thus a part of the religious leadership of the Jewish nation. He belonged to the group of non-Palestinian Jews who frequented Jerusalem. Could he have first heard the gospel at Pentecost?

Later he was to lead Saul and Mark to Cyprus for a sharing of the gospel (see 13:1-12). In Jerusalem he shared what he had, a piece of property. No strings appear to be attached to the gift. When Barnabas gave it, he gave it completely—no longer exercising control over its use. Perhaps he enjoyed giving of his material possessions so much that it was easy to give himself when the opportunity arose.

More than the enlistment of a single man was involved, however. Another result was the demonstration of true *koinonia*. The earlier account describes the church as "having favor with all the people. And the Lord added to them day by day those that were saved" (2:47). The church grew. All Jerusalem witnessed their love for one another; many longed to belong. Both spiritual and physical needs had become a deep concern of the church. God is interested in both. Why should not his church be?

2. Hypocrisy (5:1-11)

No sin in Israel deserved a stronger denunciation than did hypocrisy. Jesus rebuked the nation's religious leaders repeatedly for their insincere demonstrations. The Pharisees and their scribes were the target of much strong language. A series of woes reported in the Gospel according to Matthew (chap. 23) stands out as a summary statement of their hypocrisy. With their knowledge of the law, and their popularity with the people, the Pharisees bore heavy responsibility. Jesus noted their high moral standards and their great promise. Their high-sounding phrases, however, could not drown out the discord. They were blind guides whose actions betrayed their words. Surely the church would not fall into the sin of hypocrisy. Surely the contemporary church is on guard against this evil.

The Problem (5:1-2)

As is frequently true, the solution of one problem gave rise to another. By the sharing of possessions, the problem of economic insecurity was solved. The church's image in the community was positive. One man, Barnabas, received great acclaim because of his generosity. However, in the congregation was another man who, with his wife, Sapphira, possessed some land. Is it possible that their land possessed them?

The sharing in Jerusalem was a voluntary matter. No one was required to sell his possessions and give to the poor. Barnabas' example must have inspired others. Had the honor accorded Barnabas for his gift led Ananias and Sapphira to suppose that the church honored only those who made sizable contributions? Perhaps something—or someone—in the congregation had encouraged Ananias and Sapphira to believe that their reputations would be enhanced by a large gift. It is difficult to say when their hypocrisy began. Whatever the case, Ananias and Sapphira plotted to create an appearance of generosity, even sacrifice. Their gift would be presented, and misrepresented. A part of their land's sale price would be given as the whole of it. Thus hypocrisy entered into the church's life.

The Solution (5:3-10)

Peter charged Ananias with allowing Satan to fill his heart. (Jesus, similarly, had found the problem to be in the heart of man. See Mark 7:1-23.) Wrong attitudes and bad motivation frequently result in hypocrisy. Both the husband and wife, when confronted by the fact of their deception, suffered similar fates. Each of them fell down and died (vv. 5,10). The problem was lying church members. They had lied to the Holy Spirit.[1]

The confrontation may appear to have been particularly harsh, but neither Peter nor Luke apologized for it. Jesus had warned his hearers about a sin against the Holy Spirit. (See Matt. 12:22-37.) When the sin of Ananias and Sapphira (a high-handed, premeditated decision to deceive God) is placed in the context of the Holy Spirit, the solution is acceptable. They had sought to deceive the Author of life. It was considered God's judgment on hypocrisy. When church members are no longer able to trust one another, the life has gone out of the congregation; its witness has little effect.

The Result (5:11)

The report on Ananias and Sapphira reached beyond the confines of the church. At the least, a healthy fear of God came upon persons inside and outside the church. However, no negative reaction set in; "signs and wonders" (v. 12) done by the apostles were taken as evidence of God's presence and love. The compassion which moved Jesus to heal the sick filled his followers. Their relationship with God was free from hypocrisy; the channel of spiritual power was clear.

The church members were "with one accord" (5:12). No one appears to have departed the fellowship out of sympathy for Ananias and Sapphira. That the church met in the Temple area in great numbers suggests the problem for the Jerusalem authorities. Like a swarm of bees, these believers moved together, filling a large area by their presence.

The effect on the bystanders was striking. Some of them, unwilling for their own motives to be starkly displayed, were frightened away. Yet they talked about the church and the events, and were amazed by them. Since the Lord was drawing men and women to himself through it all, believers were added to the church. The judgment became an acted-out parable, and the people responded as Jesus had predicted; some were repelled by the harshness of truth; others were attracted. Yet truth held sway.

Hypocrisy threatens the spiritual power of any church. It is a breach of the fellowship. It violates the closeness of the relationship. If church members cannot trust one another, there is no fellowship. Such hypocrisy is best exposed by the pure motivation of the vast majority.

3. Persecution (5:17-42)

A popular maxim goes: "You can tell a man by the enemies he makes." Of course, he can be known by his friends, too, but his opposition may declare more. They fear his integrity; they know his motives. A clear-cut enmity, beyond petty hate and mere dislike, is frequently an asset. Evil is a reality in the world, and goodness repels it. If the goodness is real, opposition results. Goodness was real in Jesus; the opposition crucified him. Had he not spoken of persecution for his followers?

Evil is no less real in our day. Has the modern church accommodated itself to evil? Has its goodness become less real, less recognizable? Churches, like people, may be known by the kind of enemies they have.

The Problem (5:17-18)

The apostles' popularity, and the rapid growth of the church, presented a threat to the status quo. The Sadducees, conservative and comfortable, were set to preserve things as they were. They had been shaken by Jesus' cleansing of the Temple (Luke 19:45-48), and had responded gladly to Judas' offer (Luke 22:3-5). Their fortress of conservatism was the Temple, but now the church infested it. Never so popular with the people as the Pharisees, the Sadducees were the wealthiest sect among the Jews. They derived much of their income from the Temple system. Since selfish interests were deeply involved, their opposition was not unexpected.

When the apostles were arrested and placed in jail overnight, the reader is not surprised. From time to time in Acts this scene is repeated. You can almost tell an apostle by the sort of jails he inhabited! Such persecution as the church experienced came mainly at the hands of Jewish, not Roman, authorities. The Romans were drawn into the fray by the two religious groups, but they themselves could not have cared less about matters of doctrine. The apostles and the Sadducees did serve the same God; apparently, so did Jesus and the religious leaders. To the Romans, the Jews' religious quarrels made no sense. The Roman Empire, however, was to be kept intact, as was the peace.

The problem for the Sadducees was the apostles' popularity with the people. They had experienced, at an earlier period,

Jesus' growing popularity. The problem for the apostles was the persecution which their popularity sparked: they were in prison. Later, when released from prison, they were charged with agitation, if not insurrection (5:28). Still later, Christians were charged with divisiveness (14:4), with setting forth unlawful customs (16:20-21), with turning the world upside down (17:6), with babbling about strange gods (17:18), with law-breaking (18:13), with threatening business (19:26-27), and even with bringing Gentiles into the Temple (21:28). They continued to stir up opposition, and this opposition resulted in a long period of persecution. Why did it cease? Or did it?

The Solution (5:19-40)

Persecution will not cease when entrenched evil is threatened by goodness in human form. We are not surprised, then, to discover the persecution renewed. The scene opens in prison (5:17-18). Suddenly a messenger of the Lord (this is what the word "angel" means, and this is what an angel is) opened the doors (v. 19). The apostles stepped out of the prison and moved toward the Temple in obedience to the command, "Speak in the Temple to the people all the words of this Life" [2] (5:20).

Significantly, the apostles boldly obeyed. And in such bold obedience lies the solution to many problems. When the church or its leaders, seeking safety, turn and run from a problem, its solution is impossible. The solution to the problem of persecution is not for them to escape from it, but to obey God in spite of it.

There once was a stutterer who claimed that his speech problem had been solved. Yet he stuttered as he proclaimed his victory. He spoke, however, of God's grace in spite of his stuttering. Indeed he had solved his problem! The church located in a deteriorating neighborhood does not always solve its problems by moving out. The deteriorating neighborhood may well follow it. It simply shares God's grace with the neighborhood. In such bold obedience lay the solution to the church's problem in Jerusalem.

The high priest and the Sanhedrin had charged Peter and John "not to speak at all nor teach in the name of Jesus" (4:18). However, they had resumed their teaching in the Temple itself. The people who heard would, perhaps, turn upon members of the Sanhedrin who had taken part in Jesus' crucifixion. (See Luke 22:6 to 23:1.) In the boldness of the apostles, the Jewish leaders sensed their own defeat.

As is frequently true, God raised an ally from another quarter. Within the Sanhedrin itself was a Pharisee named Gamaliel, a

respected teacher of the law. It is not known who reported the
proceedings to Luke, but Gamaliel's wise counsel compares favorably with what is known of him. He is not described as having
preached a gospel sermon. That would have been out of character. He simply reminded the Sanhedrin of history (5:34-39).
There had been other movements in the life of the nation. They
had come to naught because they were of men. Gamaliel reasoned
that if the apostles' movement was man's work, it also would
come to nothing. Conversely, if the movement was God's work,
men—even they—were powerless to stop it. His counsel of "wait
and see" was adopted (vv. 34-40).

Josephus, in his history, mentions a Theudas who led an insurrection against the Romans.[3] Judas, who is also mentioned, very
well may have been the leader who objected to the census of A.D.
6.[4] Certainly this would fit the chronology suggested by Gamaliel.

In his recommendation to the Sanhedrin, Gamaliel gave the
apostles the benefit of the doubt.[5] Gamaliel's sympathies were
clearly with the church insofar as Luke reported. We might expect
some of the good teacher's tolerance to have rubbed off on his
best-known student, Saul of Tarsus (Acts 22:3). The zeal with
which Saul persecuted the church, however, indicates otherwise.

The Sanhedrin agreed, called the apostles in, beat them, and
charged them to be silent concerning Jesus. However, they did
not obey the charge! This was not the final solution to the
problem of persecution, but it is representative. Later (12:2),
James, the brother of John, was executed by Herod Agrippa I.
This severity, however, was unusual. Usually, God's Spirit troubled
the heart of a man, moved a mountain of opposition, or revealed
a legal escape. Whatever the case, persecution could not dampen
the enthusiasm of the church.

The Result (5:41-42)

Various responses to opposition exist. Some, preferring peace, will
be scared into silence, refusing to rock the boat. Others, having
developed a martyr's complex, will make sure that the world
knows how unjustly they have been treated. There are rare souls,
like the apostles, who rejoice in suffering for Christ's sake. Jesus
himself had declared such persons "blessed" (Matt. 5:10-12).
They came in a long line of those who had found the truth an
effective weapon. It has been suggested, partially in jest, that if
being a Christian in the twentieth century were to be declared
a crime, most would go off scot-free for lack of evidence. The
apostles counted it an honor to be recognized as Christ's people.

The togetherness in the Temple and in the homes of believers produced added strength. In recovering from arrests and beatings, the church found a new basis for fellowship and for confidence. What could possibly prevent their overwhelming Jerusalem with the good news? There is a relentlessness about these movements. ("If God *is* for us, who *is* against us?" [Rom. 8:31].) God's will will be done so long as God's people fearlessly obey the truth.

The growth of the church is indicated in 6:1 and appears to be as inevitable as before. The ability of Christians to withstand opposition excited the people, and "the number of the disciples was multiplying" (6:1). Blessed is that church whose witness is so clear that it stirs up opposition from the forces of evil! Jesus' word was fulfilled in the church's life: "Rejoice, and be exceeding glad" (Matt. 5:12).

4. Partiality (6:1-7)

A closely knit fellowship, whether Christian or otherwise, finds it easier to resist pressure from without than from within. A modern church may complete a challenging building project successfully, with ties strengthened by the spirit of sacrifice. Later, it may be tragically split over the question of admitting a member of another race or culture. Perhaps it is true of a family as well. Brothers will be as one in resisting a foe who threatens the family, but will sue one another over a small inheritance. The growing church in Jerusalem only recently successfully had solved serious problems, when "there arose a murmuring" (6:1).

The Problem (6:1)

The problem appears to have been partiality, though at its roots it may have been either pride or prejudice. There were in the church at Jerusalem few, if any, Gentiles. So the struggle did not stem from Jewish-Gentile relationships within the church. That was to come at a later time (11:1-16; 15:1-35). There were, however, various levels of culture, if not various levels of Judaism. Jerusalem was sentimentally and spiritually attractive to all Jews. Many of those born outside Palestine saved their money through young adulthood so they could move to Jerusalem, the city of David. The Temple was in Jerusalem, too, and it was the center of their faith.

These non-native-born Jews were described as Hellenists, or as Grecian Jews. They lived over almost all the Mediterranean world. Paul, for example, found Jews in every city he visited.

They were engaged in commerce or in crafts. These Jews, frequently a small minority, of necessity would mingle with the Gentiles in a manner unthinkable in Jerusalem. They spoke the language of their adopted land, sometimes neglecting their Hebrew in the home. Culturally, they would be attracted to the Greek theater and the Roman games, despite the suspicion which Jewish leaders cast on these activities. Closely related to the Gentile populace in business, they would be exposed to Gentile social circles. Clearly, these social relationships affected some Jews one way; others another. In some cases, the Gentile culture forced Jewish families to be more strict in their Judaism than the Jews of Jerusalem.

When the appeal of the Holy Land proved strong enough to draw these Jews back to Jerusalem for a festive occasion—Passover, Pentecost, or Tabernacles, they were welcomed with open arms. In Jerusalem these returning Jews were good for business, as well as religion. Many came to Pentecost from all over the world (2:5-11). From time to time they would settle in Jerusalem instead of returning to their Gentile cities. As they sought to enter social circles on a permanent basis, however, they discovered that they bore the marks of their Gentile exposure. Their Hebrew was tainted with Gentile expressions, their literary interests were broader than those of the natives, and their mingling with the Gentiles in the city was easy. Naturally, these Hellenists were suspect.

Many of them became Christians. The same cultural gap that existed in everyday life was found also in the Jerusalem church. A modern solution would be to organize another church: "Those folks never will be happy in this church." On the other hand, the one fellowship was worth preserving, and had proved attractive. Besides, there were many other Greek-speaking Jews to be reached. The church had proved especially attractive to the poor, the oppressed, the lonely, and the widowed. These people were not economic assets to the congregation, and may have had few defenders. They had been attracted, not only by the dole, but by the closeness of the fellowship. They found satisfaction for their spiritual and physical needs; they were accepted and given identity.

The more able members of the church shared their goods with the less fortunate, and no one suffered need. At least, that was how the fellowship was supposed to work. However, the Grecian Jews charged that their widows "were neglected in the daily ministration" (v. 1). Luke described the charge as a class discrimination offense. There is no defense for the partiality, from either Luke or the apostles. It was just that everyone was too busy. A group of widows belonging to a particular cultural-language group was being discriminated against. The problem could hardly be more current.

The Solution (6:2-6)

Moses' appointment of the seventy (Num. 11:10-16) to care better for his people may have offered the apostles a precedent. The apostles, clearly leading the church, called the congregation together. While the twelve in their togetherness could solve most problems, they recognized their inadequacy for this one. They decided to expand the leadership by involving other church members. Working together calls for a measure of organization, and this office called for high standards: good reputation, full of the Spirit, and wise (v. 3). Perhaps the number seven was as symbolic as the number twelve. It signified completeness to most Jews, and the symbolism would not be lost on a Jewish congregation.

The apostles' statements may not recommend them for the modern concept of the ministry. They were concerned about the needs of the Grecian widows, but had established certain spiritual priorities for themselves. Although the concept of ministry is quite broad in the New Testament (1 Cor. 12), the apostles interpreted their responsibility only in terms of preaching and praying (vv. 2,4). The suggested division of responsibility pleased the congregation (frequently referred to as the multitude), and they chose seven men.

All seven men bear Greek names. On the surface this identifies them with the Grecian faction. Their selection might have been an ideal solution, or it might have represented the disinterest on the part of the Hebrew Christians. Two of the seven, Stephen and Philip, were largely responsible for the later extension of the Christian faith. Of the others no more is related in the book of Acts. One of this unknown group is Nicolaus, the proselyte of Antioch. The later prominence of the Antioch church makes him of unusual interest. The fact that a proselyte to Judaism could become prominent in the Christian church suggests the church's progress toward resolving tensions based on culture and race.

The seven are frequently referred to as the first deacons. They are nowhere referred to as deacons in the New Testament, and the two of them later mentioned certainly did not consider their ministry confined to the church at Jerusalem. Their selection, their ordination, and their ministry does establish a noble precedent. The church traditionally has found in these verses the beginning of the office of deacon.

The ordination of these men was in line with Jewish practice, and it set them apart as ministering men. Their ministry at the tables, however, is not reported. The church's action appears to have solved the problem. No further mention of partiality can be found, although the church later faced the problem of prejudice against the Gentiles (chap. 15).

The Result (6:7)

The contribution of Stephen and Philip to the life of the church is a good fallout from the ordination of the seven. The church had risen to the challenge of a painful problem; the enlistment of two powerful leaders was the highly desirable result. The church membership grew following the solution of the problem. More men and women yielded to the sovereignty of God, and "a great company of the priests were obedient to the faith" (v. 7). These priests would be prepared for spiritual leadership, and could mean much to the growing congregation. Probably they belonged to the great group of priests in Judaism, rather than to the Temple leadership, which was known for its strong opposition both to Jesus and to the early church. Their obedience may have been an eloquent protest against the Sadducees' selfish Temple leadership. Their response to the church's move to maintain impartiality was positive. Partiality was clearly condemned in the church, and a new surge of power was the result.

This surge of power came as each problem was considered by the congregation and solved. God's Spirit possessed the membership and led them to discover solutions. Each solution was followed by the growth of the congregation. Yet each solution appears to lay the groundwork for another problem. The church was a living and growing organism, much more than a static organization. Its power lay in the life which the Holy Spirit supplied.

5. Truth for Today

The Christian fellowship which shares in the joys and the sorrows of each member is attractive to those outside. This love in action is most convincing when coupled with the spoken word of God's love. Little wonder that the congregation in Jerusalem grew rapidly!

The church has a responsibility to speak the truth in love. The two, truth and love, are not opposites, but allies. The church and its membership can stand the truth, painful though it be, if there is enough love among its members. Selfishness and greed are destructive of love, and the church must be on guard against them.

Together, under the leadership of the Holy Spirit, God's people can face the most difficult problems. The fellowship becomes stronger as it experiences the presence and the direction of God's Spirit.

God does not promise ease for his children, but he does provide courage to meet life's problems. A living and growing church may expect problems—problems for which God's Spirit has the solution.

God's love extends to all people; his people, working together, witness to that love. Human barriers of education, culture, creed, race, or politics fall before the warmth of God's love.

Frequently problems that confront the Christian fellowship may be solved by the appointment of good men, but the larger body must maintain an interest in their ministry. It is easy to charge another to express God's love in a particular situation and promptly forget it. A staff member may be charged with a ministry which a lay member ought to share. An expression of love is most effective when it clearly represents God's people working together.

[1] The translation is difficult, for what they really did was to misrepresent the Holy Spirit, to blame the Holy Spirit for their action.

[2] The words used for the faith in Acts are both interesting and incisive: "the apostles' teaching" (2:42), "this counsel, or this work" (5:38), "the Way" (9:2 and rather frequently elsewhere), "Christians" (11:26), "the disciples" (11:29), "the brethren" (14:2), "new teaching" (17:19), and "sect" (28:22).

[3] Josephus, *op. cit.,* p. 590. The Theudas incident occurred about A.D. 44, and Gamaliel's address could not be dated after A.D. 32. The appearance of the name in an historical document is interesting, but there must have been others with the name Theudas. The charge that Luke is either incorrect, or unconcerned with the order of events, is not warranted.

[4] *Ibid.,* p. 673: "A certain Galilean, whose name was Judas, prevailed with his countrymen to revolt, and said they were cowards if they would endure to pay a tax to the Romans, and would, after God, submit to mortal men as their lords." The problem is treated in detail by Frederick John Foakes-Jackson and Kirsopp Lake in *The Beginnings of Christianity,* Vol. IV (New York: Macmillan, 1933), pp. 60-62.

[5] The conditional clause, "if this counsel be of men," describes a condition undetermined as to truth or untruth. On the other hand, the clause, "if it is of God," indicates that the condition is true.

The Scattered Church:
Jerusalem to Samaria and Caesarea

Acts 6:8 to 8:40

As the crow flies, Jerusalem is not far from the cities of Samaria and Caesarea. A good map of the New Testament world shows Caesarea as a coastal city. The site of the ancient city of Samaria —which was also the name of a province—is uncertain. Roads then did not move so directly, and the way from the city of Jerusalem to Caesarea or Samaria was anything but direct.

The action in this passage begins in Jerusalem. Before the action shifts from Jerusalem, the church there had to solve certain internal problems. Some of those problems rose out of earlier actions. In all that had gone on, the church had grown in membership and strength.

Was the time ripe for outreach? Was the quality of the faith strong enough to risk sharing it with a strange culture, a different community? Had the time come for expansion? Was the fellowship able to establish a mission? While the church may have pondered questions like these, one of its members, a man of faith, moved from waiting on tables to missionary action. He decided to take seriously the teachings of the Lord and of his church. Would the church follow? Could the church work together outside Jerusalem?

1. Stephen, Faithful Witness (6:8 to 8:1)

The choice of Stephen and his six fellow table ministers appears to have solved the problems of fellowship in Jerusalem. That one of the seven, Stephen, should so quickly become the center of a new problem is disappointing, at first glance. Surely the church deserved a rest from unrest.

The Roman amphitheatre at Caesarea.

Accused and Accusers (6:8 to 7:1)
Little evidence exists that Stephen actually served tables. The
Acts account would be vastly poorer had he been confined to
that ministry. Although he might have witnessed effectively at
the table ministry, he was destined for larger things. The Greek
word translated "witness" is the word from which martyr comes.
Stephen surely proved to be a martyr. Witnessing can be a risky
business.

In deed and word Stephen witnessed. Previously described as
"full of faith and of the Holy Spirit" (6:5), he later is portrayed
as "full of grace and power" (6:8). All filled up with faith, the
Holy Spirit, grace, and power, he moved among the people. Of
course, mighty deeds resulted from the overflow of God's endowment. Any man so filled will *do* something. The men of the
synagogue tried to withstand him. When they could not, they set
up false witnesses who declared, "This man ceaseth not to speak
words against this holy place, and the law" (6:13). The long
speech in chapter 7 reveals some basis for their accusation.

His opponents were Greek-speaking Jews. There were in Jerusalem a number of synagogues.[1] Among them was a gathering
of Freedmen, Cyrenians, Alexandrians, Cilicians and other Asians.
It was a strange fellowship. What could have brought them together? (Or, perhaps, they were not actually together until Stephen
stirred them up. These defenders of Jewish orthodoxy may have
been forged together by their opposition to Stephen.) That such
non-Judean Jews were more zealous for the Temple and the law
than those who lived in Jerusalem all their lives was possible.
Why should they have come to Jerusalem from Cyrene and
Cilicia? Did business justify their return? The principal business
in Jerusalem was the Temple and its sacrificial system. They were
defensive with respect to the Temple.

When Stephen's words undermined their defenses, they bribed
witnesses to accuse him falsely before the Sanhedrin. The simple
accusation concerned what Stephen had said about Jesus: He
"shall destroy this place, and shall change the customs which
Moses delivered unto us" (v. 14). To compare this accusation
with those leveled against Jesus is interesting. The accusation
against Jesus himself, reported by Matthew and Mark, reflects
the statement Jesus had made about the temple of his body (Matt.
26:61; Mark 14:58; 15:29; see also John 2:19).

Apology: Preparation for Outreach (7:2-53)
Every great movement must have a philosophy in the background.

Stephen's defense is a statement for the basis of the church's outreach. It is a direct summary of God's dealings with his people. The speaker's premises and his illustrations were clearly heard and understood. His martyrdom was the result. His opposition did not result from his being misunderstood, but from being understood too well. Had he spoken less clearly, he might have lived to a ripe old age! Stephen's defense, which is the basis for the church's outreach, may be outlined simply:

1. God had never been confined to Jerusalem or Judea (vv.2-37).
   He appeared to Abraham in Mesopotamia (vv. 2-8).
   He was with Joseph in Egypt (vv. 9-11).
   He led Jacob into Egypt (vv. 12-16).
   He protected Moses in Egypt (vv. 17-29).
   He commissioned Moses in the wilderness of Sinai (vv. 30-35).
   He brought his people out of Egypt (vv. 36-37).
2. God had consistently been disobeyed by his people (vv. 38-43).
   They resisted Moses although he gave them God's law (vv. 38-39).
   They rejected God in favor of a golden calf (vv. 40-41).
   They refused to worship God according to his will (vv. 42-43).
3. God had provided for spiritual worship, not confined to one place or one building (vv. 44-50).
   The tabernacle symbolized God's presence with his people as they moved forward in his will (vv. 44-46).
   The Temple, however, had come to symbolize God's static position in Jerusalem (vv. 47-50).
4. God's messengers had always been resisted—from the prophets to Jesus (vv. 51-53).

Among the more telling indictments in Stephen's speech was the emphatic treatment of Moses and his experience with God outside the bounds of the Promised Land. Born in Egypt, reared in a foreign court, and exiled to the wilderness, he then received on a foreign desert mountain the law which the Jews now were jealously protecting. Even Abraham had experienced God's leadership outside Jerusalem! God is spirit and cannot be confined to a particular place or people. He is self-revealing and appears to whomever he wills, wherever, and whenever he wills. His purpose becomes clearer to those who obey his will, but it extends far beyond the confines of a single nation or generation. There have always been those who resisted his will; yet his ultimate purposes have always been accomplished. Those who have followed his will freely have, like Stephen, been caught up with a heavenly vision. Like Stephen, they may die in their obedience.

All this appears to have been understood by Luke as justifying the church's outreach beyond Jerusalem.

The source for Stephen's insight lay in his vision of the Son of man (v. 56). He saw Jesus in the position of authority at God's right hand. Although Stephen may not have been a witness *of* the resurrection, he was a witness *to* the resurrection.

In terms of the world mission of Christianity, Stephen understood that Jesus was much more than the Jewish messiah of current expectation. He sensed that the Christian faith could not be confined to a single race or locale. It had to leave the Temple and Jerusalem. Although the Temple was never intended to be a static institution, it had become just that. A part of Israel's failure was its attempt to identify salvation with "historical and earthly securities and fixtures." [2] Perhaps her history might have been different had the tabernacle never been replaced by the Temple. The tabernacle symbolized movement and progress toward God's promise. The Temple supposed that God's people had achieved God's purpose and were the apple of God's eye.

A classic prophetic appraisal of the Temple appears in Jeremiah's Temple sermon (Jer. 7:1 to 8:3). That there was a continuing rivalry between the priestly and the prophetic elements in Judaism is probable. Jesus was clearly in the prophetic tradition and suffered accordingly. Stephen was also in the prophetic tradition in his emphasis on the leadership of God beyond the confines of the Temple. The Temple and its authorities had come to represent and defend the status quo. Stephen and the non-Judean wing of the church certainly were a threat. Was the church in Jerusalem to become another Temple? Is the church in any generation in danger of becoming a static institution? A contemporary witness might level such charges against the modern church.

A Witness in Death (7:54 to 8:1)

Would Stephen be martyred as a result? The maddened mob hurled stones against him. His last recorded words comprise a prayer for forgiveness, much like Jesus' prayer for those who crucified him. Luke anticipated Saul's later conversion by recording his presence at the scene of Stephen's death. What chance did the young Pharisee have of escaping the witness? Could he ever forget the courage and the clarity of Stephen (22:20)? One man died bravely as a witness to the truth. His witness in death was as effective as his words in life. Indeed his words might not have been remembered apart from his deed. The words of the dying martyr were prophetic for the church: " 'Look,' he said, 'there is a rift in the sky' " (7:56, NEB).

That the persecution against the church, which followed Stephen's martyrdom, was inspired by the Jews in Jerusalem is significant. There is no hint that the Roman government had any part. Indeed Luke was careful in Acts to show that the decision of Roman judges consistently favored the church, or that the government was simply neutral in the church's struggles with Judaism. There was nothing contrary to Roman law in the church's doctrines. The ability of the church to live and thrive under imperial conditions reminds the modern reader of the church's nature: Her life's source is God!

Church members were scattered all over Judea and Samaria, although the apostles remained in Jerusalem. This fact may suggest sacrificial suffering on their part. It may suggest, on the other hand, that the church's outreach was the work of Greek-speaking Christians. Stephen, Philip, and, later, Saul, were apparently all non-Judean Jews, and the world mission is closely identified with them. To be sure, Peter moved out from Jerusalem as a Christian witness. However, the Jerusalem church was quick to question his efforts among the Gentiles (see 11:1-18). There were, perhaps, many persons in the Jerusalem church who breathed a sigh of relief when the troublesome Greek-speaking Jews moved out!

When the book of Acts was written, this particular persecution was past. The church, however, soon was to be confronted with another. Persecution was regarded as a challenge, an opportunity to witness. A sentence from Tertullian, a Christian writer of that period, expresses the lesson learned, "The blood of martyrs is the seed of the church." A martyr is a witness.

2. Agent of Outreach: Philip (8:2-40)

An Open Door to the Samaritans (8:2-13)
The scene shifts from Jerusalem and the scattering believers to the *city* of Samaria. The article, omitted in some manuscripts, designates the city as an important place, not simply a village. If the article is correct, the reference is to Sebaste, splendidly rebuilt by Herod the Great. If the article is omitted, the reference may be to Gitta, traditional home of Simon the sorcerer. In that city, whichever it may have been, was a particular Christian— Philip. Philip, like Stephen, could not be confined to a table-waiting ministry. He represents those who were scattered from

Jerusalem. He was not the only one. Others also were preaching the Word.

Samaritans and the Jews (shortened from Judeans) had erected barriers against one another. Traditionally, Samaritans represented the riff-raff left in the land after the noblest among them had been taken away by Sargon of Assyria in 722 B.C. The Israelites remaining had intermarried with the enemy. They resented the exiles' return to Jerusalem after the Babylonian captivity, which ended in 536 B.C. They had established their own worship center at Mt. Gerizim, a site of early historical significance (see Deut. 27). Their interpretation of Scripture marked them as religiously different from the Jews. The Gospel narratives reveal the sharp contention between the two peoples. The Samaritans worshiped in Shechem at Mt. Gerizim. They valued as Holy Scripture only the five books of Moses. They had preserved their own traditions, social customs, and hatred of the Jews. Religiously and culturally, the Samaritans rejected the Jews; and the Jews rejected the Samaritans.

For one of the apostles to approach the Samaritans would have been difficult. Matthew preserved Jesus' words on going to Israel first (see Matt. 10:6). Philip (not one of the twelve) saw an open door to the Samaritans and entered. Samaria was no problem for Philip. As in the case of Stephen, the crowd both saw what he did and heard what he said. How tragic it is when the good news is only a matter of speaking!

The healings and the good news of the Messiah's having come stirred the city to joy. Suddenly from the wing of the stage came one Simon the sorcerer. In a nonscientific age a magician thrived on superstition. Simon's reputation was made: "This man is that power of God which is called Great" (8:10). How he took advantage of their ignorance and used their loyalty is not described. Such actions were not characteristic of Philip. That Simon believed and was baptized comes as something of a surprise (v. 13). How much he believed may be indicated by his later ambitious request of Peter (v. 19).

The Church Reaching Out (8:14-25)

Meanwhile, back at Jerusalem the apostles had heard that the Samaritans had become believers. How did the Jerusalem church react? Had not James and John wanted to call down fire from heaven to destroy the Samaritans when they had rejected Jesus (Luke 9:54)? It was this same "Son of Thunder" who joined Peter in visiting Samaria. All the church became involved in outreach through the ministry of Philip. When he opened the door, he involved the church. The interested and concerned church could work together with him in his mission. Already the leaven of the gospel was expanding the minds of these Christians. Perhaps the barrier was really crossed when the apostles' prayer for them was followed by a laying on of hands. Jews touched Samaritans!

Whatever was lacking in the Samaritans' simple faith was made up by the ministry of these Jerusalem leaders (vv. 14-17). The distinction between their having been baptized into the name of the Lord Jesus, and their reception of the Holy Spirit is marked, but is not peculiar to the Samaritans. (See 19:1-6.) The Holy Spirit is free, and was not confined to the church at Jerusalem. Yet he indwelt that fellowship and led in their working together. He honored their outreach to Samaria by confirming the experience of the new believers. His coming was clearly recognizable, though neither tongues as of fire nor speaking in tongues is mentioned in this account. Perhaps the harvest of the Spirit, "love, joy, peace, etc." (Gal. 5:22-23) was manifest in the relations between Jew and Samaritan. Here was a miracle! A modern crossing of religious, racial, or cultural boundaries might as clearly be ascribed to the work of the Holy Spirit. Today's dialogue between Baptist and Catholic, Baptist and Jew, Catholic and Jew, black and white, may be the work of the Holy Spirit, and prove miraculous in their outworkings, too.

Simon's response to the Spirit's manifestations is disappointing, but underscores the reliability of the Acts account. Here is no fairy tale, with all living happily ever after. Already, a problem in the church at Samaria reared its head. Simon's attempt to purchase spiritual power (vv. 18-19) gave the name "simony" to the medieval practice of selling and buying clerical positions. The sharp rebuke of Peter, "Thou art in the gall of bitterness and in the bond of iniquity" (v. 23), reflects the shallow nature of Simon's previous response. Mystified by the marvelous, he was not yet mastered by Jesus Christ! Perhaps Luke purposely drew a sharp contrast between Simon the magician and Simon the miracle worker. However, Peter offered him repentance; and Simon asked for intercessory prayer.

Peter and John had come as messengers of the church at Jerusalem and had given the Samaritans spiritual help. Neither the church nor its leadership had run away from the problem. Nor had they broken fellowship with Philip because he led in outreach. They had confronted the work of God with people different from themselves and had accepted it as genuine. On the way back to Jerusalem, Peter and John themselves preached the good news of God's love to the Samaritans. That good news was intended for all the world.

An Opportunity with the Ethiopian Eunuch (8:26-39)

God had not yet finished with Philip. The revival in Samaria was not necessarily concluded, even though Philip was led elsewhere. From many converts, and an exciting experience, Philip was directed to a road that led south from Jerusalem. Did Philip question the divine strategy? Did Philip weigh the masses dwelling in Samaria against the few who traveled that road? Did Philip actually go through Jerusalem on his way south from Samaria? "He arose and went" (v. 27). That is obedience.

Insofar as Philip and the Holy Spirit were concerned, one other man was on that road. He was as much a reject from Judaism as were the Samaritans. Although honored by his queen, and devoted to Jewish worship at Jerusalem, he could never have become a Jew. The racial barrier was not the problem. He may have been as Semitic as Peter. The problem was that he was a eunuch.

The law plainly refused a eunuch a place in the assembly of Israel (Deut. 23:1). Nothing he could do would have changed that law. The prophet Isaiah had spoken of a day when that law would be transcended by God's gracious salvation (Isa. 56:4-5). Like many others of Isaiah's righteous pronouncements and spiritual hopes, however, this promise was ignored by first-century Judaism. A eunuch could not become a Jew. He could offer his gifts at the Temple, and long for full acceptance, but a part in the covenant was denied him. Could the gospel cross this barrier?

To imagine a more dramatic meeting, man-to-man, on the dusty road would be difficult. The eunuch, returning home, was reading from the prophet Isaiah! He had gone as far as the law allowed in Judaism. His reading of Isaiah was preparing him for the gospel. Even the Hebrew Scriptures had been translated into the Greek language. His limited exposure to Jewish life made it easier for him to believe.

The passage from which the eunuch was reading was not a popularly accepted messianic passage. Jews of the first century did not find in the image of the Suffering Servant satisfaction for their own national messianic hopes. The Christian church seized upon such passages in the Old Testament as being fulfilled clearly in the sufferings of Jesus. The Jews had rejected that kind of Messiah. Perhaps, in his loneliness and frustration, the passage from Isaiah 53 spoke clearly to the eunuch's deep need. The Old Testament Scriptures played a large part in the witness of the early church. Long after the break with the Jewish institutions, the church retained its basic interest in the Old Testament Scriptures. God spoke through them, even to the eunuch.

An interpreter, like Philip, was helpful. Among those scattered from Jerusalem there must have been others who understood and interpreted the Scriptures in this manner. Such ministry was approved by the church, and this account is preserved as a witness to the outreach of the church. The Scripture by itself is powerful, but it is understood more easily under the guidance of a Spirit-filled man.

Philip showed the eunuch how the Scripture was fulfilled in the sufferings of Jesus. In his talking about Jesus, he must have said something about Christian baptism. The eunuch was eager to be identified by baptism with God's people. Had Philip told him how the Holy Spirit frequently came to the believer in connection with baptism? Of course the Holy Spirit could come with the laying on of hands, or simply in the public worship experience. There was water by the side of the road—why not? Was his being a eunuch a hindrance?

There was no hindrance which God's grace could not remove.[3] They went down into the water and out, and "the Spirit of the Lord caught away Philip" (v. 39). Philip's response to the Spirit's leadership does not seem to have disturbed the eunuch, who "went on his way rejoicing" (v. 39). No longer was he an outcast from God's people. The church, through Philip, had reached out to include him.

All the Cities to Caesarea (8:40)
There is an interesting distinction between the villages of the Samaritans, in which Peter and John preached on their way back to Jerusalem (v. 25), and the cities in which Philip preached on his way to Caesarea (v. 40). Perhaps it is only a matter of style, but a wider offering of the gospel may be reflected in the terms. Philip settled in Caesarea, and appears on the stage again in 21:8-9 as the father of four daughters who prophesied.

3. Truth for Today

A ministry in the church is not an honorary position. Whether the member is to serve as table waiter, benevolence committee member, or stirring apologist for the faith, he is expected to function as God leads. Stephen's short ministry was varied, but effective.

God is spirit and cannot be confined by human fences. Our acceptance of his sovereignty over all creation involves our faith in his ability to reveal himself where he wills. No human group or institution controls him.

It is frighteningly easy to disobey God and deceive ourselves at the same time. Loyalty to nation, family, or even to a particular church may become more demanding than loyalty to God. Under such self-deception spiritual crimes may be committed against other persons of different nationalities or families or churches, and we may suppose ourselves to be doing God's will. The Inquisition reminds us of the excesses to which religious men may go.

An apparent tragedy may work out to God's glory. God is able to "get into the act" and bring a blessing out of a terrible disappointment; to change tragedy into a triumph. The loss of a leader in one church may mean a larger field of service in another church. A Christian need not be confined for life to one fixed area.

There is no one, except Satan, to whom the love of God is bad news. The most hopeful and the most despondent, the most attractive and the most repulsive, the most powerful and the most dependent—all want to be loved. The church offers the love of God to all men.

The Scripture bears a witness to the world, and its use ought to be encouraged. The Scripture's witness is clearer, however, when lovingly interpreted in word and deed. Mastery of the message is important. So is mastery by the Holy Spirit, who—Jesus gave the promise—is our teacher.

---

[1] It is possible that the reference is to several different synagogues. A Jewish tradition, not necessarily reliable, reported 480 synagogues in Jerusalem.

[2] William Manson, *The Epistle to the Hebrews* (London: Hodder and Stoughton Ltd., 1951), p. 35. Professor Manson has related the apology of Stephen to the Epistle to the Hebrews in an interesting and convincing fashion. His insight into Stephen's "school" is helpful.

[3] Verse 37, attractive as a Christian confession, is not included in the most reliable manuscripts of the New Testament. It appears to have been added at an early time by the church and does reflect the belief that such a Christian confession should precede baptism.

The Mission of Peter:
Judea and Caesarea

Acts 9:32 to 10:48; 12:1-24

A pastor described a man in his congregation as a diamond in the rough. On occasion this Christian was a real gem, agreeable and active. On other occasions he was stubborn and lazy. However, he was becoming more agreeable and more active. The Lord was using his fellowship with other Christians, the patience of his pastor, and the challenge of a difficult task. The beauty in the diamond was beginning to show through. How many diamonds in the rough lie about, awaiting the skilled polisher, only God knows. One of the more interesting such characters in the New Testament is Simon Peter. As a roughly cut diamond he had much promise. The polishing process began early in Jesus' ministry and continued through Peter's denial and restoration. Meanwhile, Peter learned of God's purpose in Jesus' ministry, especially in the crucifixion and the resurrection.

Peter's own ministry reached a high point with a powerful sermon at Pentecost. Simon Peter came to be remembered also for his ministering to human needs. Many recalled his personal interest in the lame man at the Temple gate and his healings in Judea. Any pastor knows a great variety in his ministry. Peter was ministering to human need, even as a good pastor does.

Some scholars have suggested entitling this section of Acts "The Acts of Peter." Peter himself would be the first to insist that it was God who did the acting. God had acted in Jesus. Peter was simply following in Jesus' steps. How wise was Jesus' choice of Peter! How effective was Jesus' training! Many New Testament scholars believe that much of the record of Jesus' ministry as found in Mark, Matthew, and Luke is based upon Peter's recollections. He had belonged to the inner circle of the disciple band. He was marked for leadership.

1. Miracles in Judea (9:32-43)

The curtain rises as Peter journeys from Jerusalem through the countryside of Judea. It would have been difficult for Peter, a Galilean, to have been confined to the Temple and the streets of Jerusalem. Others of the apostles might have stayed within the shelter of the Temple courts, but Peter was much too aggressive for that. God had some miracles to work through Simon.

Aeneas at Lydda (9:32-35)

The man Peter found at Lydda had been bedridden for eight years. This would have extended back through the ministry of Jesus certainly. Jesus had not healed all the palsied, the lame, and the feverish. Since many were left in need, his followers were empowered for the task. Perhaps Aeneas had not complained, being willing to suffer patiently. In a quiet visit Peter found him, and, through Peter, Jesus healed him. The use of the word "found" indicates Peter's interest in people. He was reaching out for people.

The church and its leadership will disappoint many if they overlook persons like Aeneas. The outreach to Aeneas and Dorcas was not motivated by the desire for a larger membership, nor a larger attendance, nor even a larger budget. The same compassion Jesus showed toward human suffering found expression in Simon Peter. So must it be with us.

Dorcas at Joppa (9:36-43)

The ancient town of Joppa, where Jonah fled from the will of God, was the scene of Peter's next ministry. What could Peter do at Joppa? That question is answered in Peter's work with Dorcas. Every ladies' Sunday School class named Dorcas memorializes this early saint. She sewed for the poor. She was missed when she died. Christ's friends grieved at her passing.

Her miraculous story is told simply and reads like an eyewitness account. Two men went from Joppa to Lydda and urged Peter to come immediately. In an informal and attractive manner Peter went to minister to a need. After his prayerful charge to Tabitha (Dorcas' name in Aramaic), she sat up—alive. Word of the miracle spread through all Joppa, and many believed. In Lydda, also, many believed because of the miracle of healing.

Although there is no record in the Gospels that Jesus had visited either town, he had set the example (see Luke 8:1). Peter was following his Lord. He was sharing the good news. He ministered where he saw need.

There is a design apparent in Luke's account. All the Judean ministry is preparatory to a larger ministry. The mission, begun in Jerusalem, was not to be confined there. Peter, ministering to the need of a palsied man, and responding to the pitiful cries of Dorcas' friends, presents us a picture of true Christian concern reaching out to meet other person's needs, wherever and whatever they are.

Further, this story tells of the gospel's startling advance in outreach. Peter stayed in Joppa with one Simon, a tanner. Tanners dealt with the hides of dead animals, some of which were ceremonially unclean (see Lev. 11:39-40). Simon the tanner must have been beyond the pale of Jewish ceremonial law. Yet Peter stayed with him. And then, Joppa was on the road from Lydda to Caesarea, where the Gentile Cornelius lived. Why did Luke include these facts, if not to suggest the ever widening circles of gospel concern?

2. A Miracle in Caesarea (10:1-48)

From the country towns of Judea the scene of the Acts changes abruptly. Caesarea, a Gentile city, was destined to become quite significant in early Christian history. This seaport, built by Herod the Great, was large enough to serve seagoing vessels. Even now the extensive harbor construction is visible. The port city became the Roman capital of Palestine and enjoyed the cultural advantages of a Roman city. Here the Roman governor lived in a palace built by Herod. From Caesarea the ruler journeyed to Jerusalem, where at festive seasons he asserted his authority by his presence. Since the population of Caesarea was predominantly Gentile, the relations between Jew and Gentile were not always smooth. Caesarea appears to have been the center of emperor worship, although the presence of many Jews would have insured that synagogues also were there.

A Gentile at Prayer (10:1-8)

Among the Gentiles in the city was Cornelius, a centurion, who was also a God-fearer. Always the New Testament treats centurions with respect. These responsible Roman soldiers were not subject to the excesses of high-ranking military officers. The strength of the legions rested on their shoulders. They were chosen with this in mind. As a God-fearing Gentile, Cornelius was closely related to Judaism. He had been attracted, as had many Gentiles, to its worship of one God and its ethical ideals.

When the scene opens in Caesarea, Cornelius is at prayer. The spiritual influences of Jewish teachings and practices were stronger than often supposed. His continual prayers were accompanied by generous gifts. Thus he was ready for God's further revelation. He wanted to know what else a Gentile could do to approach the God of Israel.

The God of grace responded to the centurion's practical faith. Cornelius had no reason to know Simon Peter. He may have known nothing of the ministry of Jesus. He had respect for Judaism, however, and feared God. When he clearly understood God's will, he made arrangements to obey. He shared his vision with two servants and a soldier, and sent them to Joppa.

A Jew at Prayer (10:9-23)

While God's charge to the Gentile was being obeyed, Peter was praying. He also was a man of spiritual habit. His faith had been challenged by recent events, and he was seeking the Lord's direction. For many days he had stayed at Joppa, waiting.

While he prayed, about noontime, he became hungry. The vision concerned food, but it was unclean food. The Jewish law was quite detailed in its distinctions between clean and unclean food (see Lev. 11:1-45). Not only were certain animals unacceptable as food, but even acceptable animals were to be slaughtered so as to bleed properly (Lev. 17:10-14). Gentiles, on the other hand, delighted in rare cuts. That a good Jew should even dream of eating unclean food was absurd! Peter was troubled by his vision.

Yet during his ministry Jesus had made "all meats clean" (Mark 7:14-23). Some scholars believe that the Gospel of Mark represents Peter's memories of Jesus' ministry. Does Mark 7:14-23 relate to this encounter? When did Peter fully recognize the meaning of Jesus' words? After his practical experience with them? How does one come to understand the Word of God? Later Peter would remember Jesus' words in the light of his own experience with the Gentiles and conclude that this was God's intention from the beginning. At first, however, Peter defended himself as a law-abiding Jew: "I have never eaten anything that is common and unclean" (v. 14).

Three times the strange vision came. Each time the express command of the Lord directed Peter to act in defiance of the law. For a Jew to see God's direction as supreme over the law was difficult. When God's people cannot accept God's will for them because it challenges their past understanding, the result can be tragic. Such a static approach to God's will has made following God's leadership difficult for many Christians. God's charge to Peter was not in violation of the law; it rested on God's authority over the law. Peter was troubled by the vision.

While Peter considered the disturbing vision, God was moving to make its meaning clear. The three men sent by Cornelius were already at the house. A decision which might have caused Peter great anxiety now became clear because of God's preparation. Peter invited the two household servants and the soldier into the house and entertained them. While at prayer, both Cornelius and Peter had sensed God's will.

A Jew Preaching to a Gentile (10:23-43)

Jonah had heard the Lord call at Joppa, too. How much earlier Jonah had understood his mission to Nineveh, or where he had first sensed God's will, the ancient narrative does not reveal. Joppa was the scene of his disobedience. He rejected the concept of God's love for the non-Israelite. He refused to be the arm of God's outreach to the world beyond. Joppa might well have been the site of Peter's disobedience, too, and of the church's refusal to reach out. But it was not.

Fortified by prayer, Peter accompanied the visitors to Caesarea. That he took some of his friends from Joppa with him is significant (v. 23). He was wise enough to know that the church at Jerusalem would frown on his mission to a Gentile household. Had not Jesus admonished his disciples to be "wise as serpents and harmless as doves" (Matt. 10:16)? Before Pentecost such a mission would have been unthinkable for Peter.

The friendly tour of Judean towns and the healing of a few sick merely furnished the backdrop for the change of direction toward Caesarea. It was but the prelude to the main action. Was the church ready to reach out to a Gentile with the gospel? There was no time for the church in Jerusalem to call a conference about the matter. Peter responded to the challenge, although it appears that he was conscious of the threat to the fellowship at Jerusalem. The conference would come later, after the Holy Spirit had acted.

The foresight of both Peter and Cornelius is significant. While Peter arranged for Jews from Joppa to accompany him, Cornelius invited Gentile friends in to hear Peter. Introductions were kept to a minimum. Only brief words about the leadership of God were necessary. Peter was on the defensive about being in the house of a Gentile, but he had crossed the barrier. Cornelius' explanation was more detailed: He had been directed by God to summon Peter (vv. 30-33). All things were ready. Peter began to preach.

From an Old Testament mission concept (Deut. 10:17; 2 Chron. 19:7) Peter took his text: "God is no respecter of persons" (v. 34). The Greek phrase, literally translated, means "God does not receive a man's face," or "God does not take man at his face value." God is concerned with the inner man rather than the outer appearance. It was quite an experience for Peter. He recognized it as the logical outgrowth of Christ's own mission (vv. 34-43). At the outset he admitted that one who feared God and worked righteousness was acceptable to God. Was he describing Cornelius? Peter's statement in verses 34-35 is a summary of one of the prophetic insights of the Old Testament prophets. (See, for example, Isa. 49:5-6.) However, few of the prophets had been held in honor until after death. Their missionary messages were simply filed under the proper heading.

Peter summarized Jesus' ministry with the beautiful statement, "Jesus . . . went about doing good" (v. 38). Verse 37 may imply that Cornelius had prior knowledge of that ministry, although no record that Jesus preached in Caesarea exists. Jesus' healing ministry is described as a conquest of the devil (v. 38). Jesus' ministry, Peter asserted, was performed in the power of the Holy Spirit. Peter himself had witnessed these events (v. 39).

Apostolic preaching did not fail to recount the passion. The apostles were dismayed at the rejection of God's Son by Israel. The details of the rejection, the betrayal, the trial, the denial, the crucifixion, and the resurrection were etched forever on Peter's mind and heart. He recounted them over and over. This fact is clear in the close agreement of the four Gospels on these events. Each of the Gospel writers approached Jesus' last days in a different manner, but a close similarity exists in their reports of the passion events. Jesus' death and resurrection was the core of the good news, the heart of the gospel. In these events is the clearest manifestation of God's love in Christ.

Peter's sermon continued through the resurrection (v. 41), for without this triumph of love and life all else would have meant nothing. Nor was the sermon a secondhand report. All the events, including the resurrection, were a part of Peter's personal experience. God had chosen him and certain others. Their mission was clear: Preach to the people. The theme of judgment was also an essential part of the good news, but details on the judgment are omitted (v. 42). The invitation was as broad as the human race: "Every one that believeth" (v. 43).

The Holy Spirit and Gentiles (10:44-48)

The coming of the Holy Spirit is not confined to any particular event in the life of God's people. Nor, to Peter's surprise, is his coming confined to any particular sort of people. Peter had taken, perhaps with reluctance—certainly with questions, the gospel to the house of a Gentile. Peter did not know what to expect as a result of his obedience. Caesarea, rather than Pentecost, may have been Peter's noblest hour. God sent his Spirit upon the Gentiles, and the Jews present were amazed. How about Peter?

He interpreted the gift as confirmation of their faith. The manifestation, including the "tongues" of praise, was evident to all. Peter's reference to baptism for the Gentiles may appear to be a bit defensive: "Can any man forbid the water?" (v. 47). This question only emphasizes that Caesarea was a real breakthrough. (The later attitude of the church at Jerusalem marks his reaction as realistic [see 11:1-3].) The Gentiles were baptized "in the name of Jesus Christ" (v. 48).

3. A Miracle in Jerusalem (12:1-24)

The phrase, "Now about that time" (12:1), introduces another striking experience in Peter's ministry. The smooth flow of events in these chapters has behind them the writer's art, guided by God's Holy Spirit. In the Gospel, Luke grouped his materials around certain mighty movements, as, for example, the travel narrative for Jesus' journey to Jerusalem (Luke 9:51 to 19:28). Luke's organization of that material suggests a similar plan here. We move from event to event, each one building on the other. Peter's release from prison and Herod's eventual death seem to explain verse 24: "But the word of God grew and multiplied." Among other purposes Luke had in writing Acts, this goal seems clear: to show how Christ's mission expanded through the faithful witness of his followers. (Similar verses mark the developing theme [see 2:47; 4:4,31; 5:11,42; 8:4; 9:31].)

The Execution of James (12:1-2)

Acts 12 is filled with marvels. The Herod of this chapter was a personal antagonist to the church. His grandfather was Herod the Great, best known for his slaughter of the infants in Bethlehem (see Matt. 2:16). (Herod the Great also slew his wife Mariamne and their son Aristobulus. Aristobulus was this Herod Agrippa's father.) [1] Agrippa was brought up in a climate of suspicion, cruelty, and gross immorality.

He had received from the Roman emperor certain predominantly Gentile territories north and east of the Sea of Galilee. Later, due to political intrigue and to the death of Emperor Tiberius, he received the kingship and the territories of Galilee,

Samaria, and Judea.[2] His power depended solely on Rome, and his relations with the Jews reflected his own political ambitions. Opposition to the church seemed an attractive political stance. His own spiritual life was negative, and his persecution certainly represented no basic Jewish loyalties.

Doubtless, the outreach from Jerusalem, and the resultant relations between Jew, Samaritan, and Gentile members, had made the church in Jerusalem somewhat repulsive to the other Jews. Herod's opposition holds no suggestion of organized Roman persecution. He was a mean man who had no conscience about killing for personal gain. What did he hope to gain? The execution of James "pleased the Jews" (vv. 2-3). Unlike Stephen, who fell to mob violence, James fell as a political pawn, sacrificed to Agrippa's ambition.

The Arrest of Peter (12:3-11)

The season was Passover; many Jews were visiting Jerusalem. Roman security was notably tight during the festive season. Peter was placed in maximum security, but the church was praying for him earnestly. Prayer proved to be the greater force. Herod had planned to give Peter to the people, much as Pilate had given Jesus to the people. He would be a post-Passover sacrifice. But God had other plans.

The scene in the prison is not unlike a later scene in Philippi (see 16:23-26). Indeed Luke appears to have compared the ministries of Peter and Paul purposely. He saw interesting and significant comparisons between the apostle to the Jews and the apostle to the Gentiles.

The spotlight focuses on the cell where Peter slept, chained to two soldiers. Other soldiers kept the door of the prison. A messenger of the Lord was present to free Peter from his chains and to lead him out of the prison into the city beyond. Peter's deliverance, according to his own account, was a miracle: "Now I know of a truth, that the Lord hath sent forth his angel" (v. 11).

A Prayer Meeting (12:5,12-16)

Meanwhile, in the house of Mary, the mother of John Mark, many were praying for Peter (vv. 5,12). Were they praying for his release? his merciful and speedy execution? his courage under fire? for the will of the Lord to be done? How does one pray under such circumstances? Their prayers were answered even while they prayed. God does move on his own schedule; to answer our prayers, he does not always wait for the "Amen."

Rhoda's behavior is delightful, and is surely evidence of the firsthand witnesses whom Luke consulted. While Peter knocked for admittance, Rhoda tried to convince his friends their prayers had been answered (vv. 14-16). That they were not expecting his release is clear, although they may have been praying for it. "It is his angel," the praying Christians concluded hopelessly (v. 15). Already, they thought, Herod had executed him, and they might as well stop praying. Luke's language is restrained: "They saw him, and were amazed" (v. 16). Luke mentioned the location of the prayer meeting—Mary's house—in anticipation of her son Mark's significance in the Christian mission at a later time. What effect was the answered prayer in Peter's behalf to have on John Mark?

"Go tell . . . James" (12:17)

The masterfully drawn narrative must be read carefully. Not only has John Mark been introduced in this scene, but a turn of events with respect to James is also noted. James, the brother of the Lord, is mentioned here. He would assume leadership of the church in Jerusalem later. Luke marked James' emergence as a leader with Peter's charge. James represented the conservative Jewish Christian wing of the church. Tradition has marked him as pious and law-abiding. Peter left in his hands the responsibility for church leadership. There is no evidence that James encouraged outreach from Jerusalem. He does not appear to have been active in witnessing. Perhaps his tasks were purely administrative. He was highly respected by the Jews in Jerusalem.

Vindication of the Church (12:18-24)

Herod reacted to Peter's escape like the tyrant he was. He ordered the execution of the soldiers who had been charged with keeping Peter. Then Herod returned to Caesarea, center of Roman authority in Palestine. His true colors are portrayed in his relations with Tyre and Sidon. The two cities represented the Phoenician culture, and regularly were grouped by the Romans with Syria, rather than Palestine. The account tells of an ancient exercise in dollar diplomacy. Herod used the food supply as leverage for personal glory. Members of the church at Jerusalem, still smarting from the execution of James and the arrest of Peter, saw in Herod's death the Lord's hand. An early Jewish historian, Flavius Josephus, placed Herod's death at A.D. 44.[3]

The triumph of the church in her faithfulness to Christ's mission is—as we have seen—one of the themes of Acts. This theme introduces the section beginning with 9:31 and concluding with 12:24. Peter's mission, from Jerusalem to Caesarea and back, is

the story. The fulfillment of Christ's mission through the witness
and ministry of faithful Christians is emphasized. Certain pre-
cedents were established in these events, which served as guide-
lines for later expansion. To see that the Jewish wing of the church
was also active in the outreach from Jerusalem is important. Luke
would be unwilling to ascribe outreach to the Greek-speaking
Christians alone, although they seem to have been involved in it
deeply. Jesus' own ministry was extended in the outreach of
Peter. To have more detail on Philip's ministry in Caesarea would
be interesting. Could he, in some sense, have prepared the way for
Cornelius' vision? The offering of the gospel to Cornelius certainly
represents an advance over previous outreach. Philip's witness to
the eunuch appears to have prepared the way, although no observers
are mentioned (8:26-39). In contrast, Cornelius' conversion was
observed by several Jewish Christians (10:23-24).

Peter's vision on the housetop must have struck a responsive
chord in Luke's mind, particularly since Luke was a Gentile. The
fellowship at Antioch was threatened when Jews and Gentiles ate
together (Gal. 2:11-14). Eating together was a real barrier to
close Jewish-Gentile relationships. Therefore Peter's vision appears
to have had a wider application than for just the household of
Cornelius.

There is perhaps a sad note in Peter's departure from Jerusalem.
Had he remained as a leader in the church there, Paul's mission
might have received more enthusiastic support. With the offering
of the gospel to Cornelius, Peter became an ally of advance. He
had moved from Jerusalem to Samaria to Judea to Caesarea.
The geographical journey was not great, but the outreach of the
church toward the Gentile world far exceeded the number of
miles Peter had traveled.

4. Truth for Today

Ministry is a means for making known the gospel. Peter's experience with Aeneas and Dorcas suggests the importance of ministry
in a gospel witness. Jesus' and Peter's example of concern for the
whole man is the pattern for Christians today. Since persons are
affected by their life situations, suffering, and the like, ministering
is an important part of the total witnessing task.

Our knowledge of God's will is subject to new understandings.
Peter thought he knew God's will. It was stated in the law. However, God found a means for enlarging Peter's understanding of

his will. That Peter moved cautiously is evidence of his uncertainty in this newfound understanding. That he moved at all is evidence of his sincerity. He wanted to know and do God's will.

Doing God's will may take courage. Peter would have had less personal stress had he backed away from Cornelius. But Peter had the courage of his convictions.

However, he also had the courage to let his understanding of God's will be subjected to the church's scrutiny. When one has a different insight, and believes that it is from God, he ought not shrink from submitting it to fellow Christians for their testing of its validity.

God's will for churches is that they reach out to people in all conditions and of all classes. This is the basic truth of this section of Acts. Peter learned that lesson; the Jerusalem church accepted it—as we shall see. However, we shall also see that not all the New Testament Christians were ready to accept the full implications of that truth.

The validity of a church's life can be measured by this truth.

God is sovereign and presides over history. Despite all the dangerous Herods of human experience, God reigns. There is no joy manifest in Luke's description of Herod death. Early Christians looked beyond present troubles to God's promised triumph. In Peter's release and Herod's defeat may be seen promise of God's future.

---

[1] A.H.M. Jones, *The Herods of Judaea* (Oxford: Clarendon Press, 1938), pp. 184-216.

[2] George Ernest Wright and Floyd Vivian Filson, eds., *The Westminster Historical Atlas to the Bible* (Philadelphia: The Westminster Press, 1945), pp. 75-76.

[3] Josephus, *op. cit.,* p. 582.

The Developing Crisis:
Damascus, Antioch, and Beyond

Acts 9:1-31; 11:19-30; 12:25 to 14:28

Stephen's death seemed to resolve possible differences within the church. The leaders may have thought Peter impulsive, but his outreach to Gentiles, such as Cornelius, could be controlled. Barnabas they considered to be all compassion; he could be expected to give ground for the sake of peace. The only cloud on the horizon of the church's inner peace was the new convert, Saul of Tarsus. How would his conversion affect the church?

1. The Conversion of Saul (9:1-31)

From the record it is clear that Saul was a Hellenistic Jew. The city of Tarsus was a large, cosmopolitan center, situated on major trade routes. Its population numbered 500,000. A Jew in such a city would have his mental and moral powers continually challenged. That Saul was sharpened by his contacts with Greek culture is clear in the New Testament record.

As a Hellenistic Jew he was bilingual. All the resources of Greek literature were his, but he appears to have spent much of his study time in the Greek translation of the Hebrew Scriptures. He was also a Pharisee. His training under Gamaliel in Jerusalem offered superb opportunity for mastering Judaism.

Another advantage which Saul enjoyed was his Roman citizenship, which allowed him a degree of security, as well as freedom of movement throughout the empire. Citizenship was a valuable asset, and many paid dearly for it. Saul was born a citizen of Rome, and this fact underscores the importance of his family background, about which indeed little is known.

Saul the Persecutor (9:1-2)
Saul is described as "breathing threatening and slaughter against

the disciples of the Lord" (9:1). The intensity with which he accepted the challenge of the church is suggested in that phrase. Why should the capable Pharisee adopt such an attitude? Although he had been present at the stoning of Stephen (7:58), he appears to have assumed a passive role. Almost immediately thereafter, however, he became active in the persecution. We know he became more zealous about the time the believers scattered from Jerusalem (see 8:1; 9:1).

Many interesting theories have sought to explain Saul's ferocious attack. One theory suggests Saul's frustration with legal righteousness, a frustration which drove him to distraction.[1] It was not that the messiah had not come. Rather, the problem was that he had come to the wrong kind of people. The Jews expected the messiah, and Saul could accept that. To suppose, however, that the messiah had come to people like Peter and Matthew—to the common people of Judaism—was more than he could stomach. Had he come to the Pharisees, Saul could have accepted Jesus. The assertion that the messiah had come to those on the fringe of the law, was, on the other hand, incredible. Not only was the assertion incredible; it was maddening.

"It would be surprising if such a man had adopted a cautiously balanced neutrality, as perhaps his teacher Gamaliel did (Acts 5:34), in the face of the Christian movement that was rising from quite different social circles: Paul had to take up a position; he did so, and became a persecutor of the Christians." [2] Some of the Pharisees tended toward the Zealot position and actively sought absolute compliance with the Jewish law. Frequent uprisings against the Romans, or attacks upon compromising Jews, disturbed the peace of calmer scribes. Saul's nephew was close enough to such a group of Zealot plotters to report the plan against Saul's life (23:12-16). Is it possible that the family was influenced by this wing of Pharisaism?

Many of the members of the Jerusalem church had fled the city following the stoning of Stephen (8:4; 9:31). Luke described this dispersion in the report of Philip's outreach. Luke also mentioned that the dispersed Cyprians and Cyrenians in Antioch offered the gospel freely to Gentiles (11:20). Simon Peter, although not a Hellenist, must also have been a target for the more zealous Jews.

Saul shared in the persecution of the church in Jerusalem (8:3). When that persecution abated (9:1-2), he took steps to stamp out the movement elsewhere. Damascus had a large Jewish population, and was a natural haven for church members leaving

Jerusalem. Although the high priest had no political power in Damascus, his influence was great. Letters from him to Jewish synagogue leaders there would insure cooperation with his wishes. Even those on the fringe of Judaism would respect an order from the high priest. Therefore, "breathing threatening and slaughter" (9:1), Saul secured such letters for his journey to Damascus.

Transformation (9:3-9)

Among the several accounts in the New Testament of the effect of Saul's conversion, no account is more forceful than the simple statement in his letter to the churches of Galatia, "They only heard say, He that once persecuted us now preacheth the faith of which he once made havoc" (Gal. 1:23). To supplement Luke's account of that conversion in Acts 9, we have the testimonies in Acts 22:3-21 and Acts 26:9-18. There is also the clear statement in 1 Corinthians 15:8, "He appeared to me." There are some unique features in each account, but there is basic agreement.

Saul was journeying toward Damascus, bent on arresting church members. About midday (Acts 22:6; 26:13), a bright light brought him to the earth, and he heard a voice saying, "Saul, Saul, why persecutest thou me?" (9:4; 22:7; 26:14). Those who were with him heard the sound, but did not comprehend it (9:7). Saul knew that it was Jesus who spoke to him; that conviction never weakened. Saul saw the Lord, and addressed him so.

Only in Paul's defense before Agrippa is reference made to the "goad" (26:14) or "pricks" (KJV). Yet here is an incisive look at the conversion experience. Goads were used by herdsmen, such as drivers of oxen, to urge livestock on. To kick at such sharp sticks was a painful experience. How long Saul had been kicking at such pricks we cannot know, but the experience had driven him to a frenzied attack on the Christian church. Certainly his growing sense of Judaism's failure, including his own frustration with the law, had led him to zealous persecution. And yet he must have grieved in his own sensitive spirit about the hopelessness of it all.

The reports on the ministry of Jesus must have pricked Saul. Jesus' compassion was undeniable, and his teachings certainly would have provoked Saul's thought. That such a one could be crucified by the Romans at the prodding of Jewish leaders would have caused him pain. In a blinding light Saul saw with clear spiritual vision: Jesus was alive! He could give up the painful battle against an incredible messiah.

Many of the Christians whom Saul arrested reacted as Stephen did—with a prayer for forgiveness. These experiences too would have goaded Saul in the direction of Christian faith. How do you attack the heresy of a good man who prays for you while you disagree violently? How many actually sought to persuade Saul to accept Jesus is unknown, but many were willing to be arrested for their faith. Their courage was evidence of their Christian assurance.

Stephen's death served as quite a painful goad. Saul had witnessed his stoning. He must have heard Stephen's strong witness. Its logic was sound. Stephen's death did not stop the relentless advance of God's truth upon Saul's defenses. Stephen's manner of death emphasized the gospel truth he had proclaimed and by which he had lived and died. It was indeed hard for Saul to kick against that goad.

Jesus' appearance to Saul was, according to the apostle's own account, an act of God's grace, specially designed for Saul. The experience was intensely personal. The ensuing blindness allowed Saul several days for deep inward search for the meaning of his vision. His entire previous life, and all its stern legalism, came crashing down. Jesus was alive! His ministry had been vindicated by God himself! The full meaning of the cross took a while to comprehend; his present ideas would need to be revised. Yet at that moment he yielded consciously to divine love; his inward eye caught sight of an entire world—both Jew and Gentile—that needed this love.

An Unwilling Witness (9:10-19)

Who would have heard of Ananias apart from his ministry to Saul of Tarsus? He is described only as "a certain disciple" (v. 10). However, he was sensitive to God's leadership. Because of that, we know about him.

Specific directions were given Ananias to go to Straight Street, to the house of Judas (v. 11). No misunderstanding of the directions was possible. God had prepared Saul by a vision, just as he was preparing Ananias. When God revealed the mission, however, Ananias was less than anxious to confront Saul of Tarsus (vv. 13-14). That Ananias knew of Saul's purpose in coming to Damascus indicates Ananias' courage; he moved to meet Saul's need.

Saul's reputation was widely known—both at Damascus and at Jerusalem. Believers feared his persecution. To Ananias God spoke of Saul's mission to the Gentiles (9:15), and the noble Christian made the point clear to Saul (22:15). Central to Saul's mission was the conviction that God's love, like his sovereignty, extended to the Gentile world. After Ananias had witnessed to Saul, Saul's sight was restored. With the promise of the Holy Spirit, he arose and was baptized. Both Ananias and Saul must have been amazed at the turn of events.

Ministry at Damascus (9:19-25)

The order of events just after Saul's baptism is not clear. (See 9:19-30; 22:17-21; 26:19-20; Gal. 1:15-21.) Paul's own account has been preserved in Galatians, in which the apostle wrote, "Before God, I lie not" (Gal. 1:20). There Paul indicated that his immediate post-conversion ministry was in Arabia and Damascus. "Arabia" might have referred to one of two places, the region or the city. The meaning is not clear. Damascus had long enjoyed the position of a semi-independent city under the emperor. About the time of Saul's conversion a political deal between Tiberius, the emperor of Rome, and Aretas, king of Arabia, appears to have placed the city under Aretas' protection. It is important to note that Arabia was a large desert kingdom, bound on the north by the Euphrates River, the east by the Persian Gulf, the south by the Indian Ocean, and the west by the Red Sea. Although it is attractive to assign Saul to a long journey to Sinai following his conversion, as some scholars do, he could have been in Arabia by stepping outside the Damascus gate.

Certainly he used his time wisely in meditation, as well as in active witnessing. The Galatians' account marks this period as extending for three years. Saul preached in many of the synagogues in Damascus. As a result, he was the subject of much discussion: A Christian persecutor had become a Christian preacher!

His message in Damascus appears to have centered on Jesus, both as Son of God and as the Messiah. This strong conviction was central to his conversion experience. In a unique manner Jesus was related to God. In a unique way Jesus was related to man. The next step for Saul was his insistence that Jesus, as Messiah, was related to all men, not just to the Jews. The opposition at Damascus may have developed when he proclaimed this.

The opposition of the Jews to Paul's ministry was to be repeated many times in the years to come. When the Damascene Jews plotted to kill him, he learned of it and was able to escape. A brief reference to the event occurs in 2 Corinthians 11:32-33 where a list of his sufferings for the gospel occurs. Apparently his abrupt and undignified departure through the walls was embarrassing to Saul (who is called Paul beginning with Acts 13:9, at Paphos). Aretas IV was king, and exercised sovereignty outside Damascus. He would have been interested in granting the request, made by some of the Jews in Damascus, that the "renegade" Saul be seized. His men watched the gate to the city carefully, thereby imprisoning Saul within (v. 25). The proclamation that Jesus was the Son of God, and the proof that he was the Messiah, was too much for the Damascene Jews.

Ministry at Jerusalem (9:26-31)

Finally (Gal. 1:18-20), Saul went to Jerusalem. There he tried to join the disciples, but they proved less than receptive to the former persecutor. Only under the sponsorship of Barnabas was Saul received by the church. Barnabas vouched for Saul's conversion and Damascus ministry. Word of that ministry must have reached Jerusalem before Saul arrived, since—according to the Galatians' passage—he had worked in Galatia for three years.

Saul joined the group of Christians in Jerusalem. As he had preached "boldly in the name of Jesus" in Damascus (9:27), so he preached in Jerusalem (9:28-29). Apparently, opposition to his bold preaching arose when he began disputing with the Grecian Jews. They were Hellenists; Saul himself was a Hellenist. His own background in Tarsus, buttressed by his Pharisaic training, and undergirded by Jesus' appearance to him, made Saul a feared foe in debate. When the Grecian Jews lost the argument to Stephen, they stoned him. When they lost the argument with Saul, they sought to kill him (v. 29). His friends took him down to Caesarea, and he returned to Tarsus (v. 30).

This period of fifteen days (Gal. 1:18) in Jerusalem must have been of great value to Saul. He had the opportunity of close fellowship with its leaders: Simon Peter, and James, the brother of Jesus. Details of the ministry of Jesus, known only to the twelve, Saul must have learned from Peter. Details of Jesus' family life, known only to family members, he may have learned from James. Paul later made clear, however, that authority for his Gentile mission was not received from them (see Gal. 2:5-9). He declared his authority and gospel came from God.

What did Saul do, once back in Tarsus? Was he quiet during the years of his stay there? The Scripture is silent at this point, except for a brief reference in 11:25. Meanwhile the church in Jerusalem—without the disturbance provoked by the Grecian Jews, Stephen, and Saul—enjoyed peace.[3] The summary statements recurring in Acts (see 2:43-47; 4:4,32-35; 5:41; 6:7; 9:31) are designed to rest the mind of the reader, as well as describe the church's respite after dramatic developments. At this time (9:31) the Jerusalem church's ministry appears to have been limited to Judea, Samaria, and Galilee. The time was ripe for reaching out to the world beyond.

2. Gentile Christians at Antioch (11:19-30; 12:25)

The center for the gospel's expansion moves at this point from Jerusalem to Antioch of Syria. (We have traced out Peter's experience in Caesarea in chapter 4.) In the establishment of this new center, the church leaders were soon confronted with a basic problem: Is the Christian gospel for all—the Gentile, as well as the Jew? The answer to that question and its meaning for us is an exciting and thrilling story.

Antioch was the capital of the province of Syria and the chief city of the eastern Mediterranean world. As the third largest city in the Roman Empire it attracted commercial interests from a large area. Since the governors of Syria were traditionally of a high quality, relations between Jew and Gentile usually were peaceful. Many of the Gentiles, having been attracted to Judaism, became proselytes.

A Martyr and Witness (11:19-21)

The events described at Antioch go back to a time shortly after the death of Stephen. News of the events in Antioch likely reached Jerusalem shortly after Saul's departure for Tarsus. Others besides Philip were scattered by the persecution following Stephen's martyrdom (8:1-5). Jews were living in many nearby areas. Believers, journeying as far as Phoenicia and Cyprus, shared the gospel with these Jews. Some, perhaps, while on their way to Cyprus, preached to Gentiles also (11:20).[4]

Thus Stephen's martyrdom resulted in an extension of the good news. The Gentiles, for the first time, openly were invited to accept the gospel and believe in the Lord Jesus. These Gentiles doubtlessly had been cultivated by Judaism, and many may have been on the verge of becoming proselytes. In other cities, this apparent competition for Gentile converts on the part of Jew and Christian provoked crises. In Antioch, on the other hand, relationships between Jew and Gentile were particularly good. The mission to Antioch was clearly unauthorized; no names are mentioned of those who first preached there. The resultant Jewish-Gentile Christian group enjoyed fellowship quite naturally, and probably did not break violently with the synagogue.

A Church at Antioch (11:22-26)

Word came to Jerusalem about the conversion of the Gentiles in Antioch. Previously a new congregation in Samaria had received a helpful visit from Peter and John (8:14). Acting on that precedent, Barnabas, of good reputation in the Jerusalem church (4:36-37), was sent to Antioch (11:22). The mission was a diplomatic move, not an official discipline.

As Peter had reacted warmly to the Gentiles in the house of Cornelius, so Barnabas responded to the Gentiles of Antioch. He saw what the Lord had done, and did not delay in sharing their attractive and open fellowship. In reading these chapters of Acts, one might be critical of the church at Jerusalem. However, we must keep in mind the fact that Barnabas was their representative. The Jerusalem church was involved in this Gentile ministry through Barnabas' work.

Under Barnabas' initial ministry the church grew. Thinking about possible helpers, Barnabas remembered Saul of Tarsus, the young man whom he had sponsored at the Jerusalem church some time before. Tarsus was near Antioch, and Barnabas brought Saul to Antioch. For a year they labored together, enjoying the fellowship of Jew and Gentile alike. A brief reference in Paul's Galatian letter (2:12) indicates that Barnabas and Saul ate with the Gentiles as a matter of course.

One of the things for which Antioch is known is that the word "Christian" first was used with reference to believers in that city. Out of respect for the name of Christ, the believers themselves likely would not have adopted the name. The Jews in Antioch would not have profaned the name of the Messiah. The title may have arisen from local gossip: Those people are always talking about Christ. The Greek word for Christ was frequently confused with a word meaning "useful." Could the public in Antioch simply have coined a nickname for these good folks?[5] The description of the Antioch believers, found in verse 26, serves as a summary statement, and as the prelude to the next developments.

A Missionary Challenge (11:27-30; 12:25)

The early church, like certain Jewish groups, was open always to the prophetic word. The prophets of ancient Israel were highly respected in Judaism. To the Jewish-Gentile church at Antioch came Agabus in the company of other prophets. The threat of famine was always real and deadly to Judea. Bad weather, or even the unwillingness of farmers to plant because of a difficult political situation, could be responsible for a poor crop. Agabus predicted a famine over all the known world. The precise date of the famine is uncertain, although there are references to a serious famine about this time. A possible reference to this famine may be found in the account of Herod's last oration (12:20).

Others are known to have aided Jerusalem in famine conditions. Some of these gifts probably helped the Christians, as well as the non-Christians. The generous spirit of the Antioch church may be seen in its prompt response: someone was in need; they sent relief by their leaders. The word translated "relief" (v. 29) may be more clearly translated "ministry."

Little concerning the visit of the Antioch party to Jerusalem appears in the Acts account (11:27-29). The gifts were given to the leaders of the congregation in Jerusalem. Acts then tells of Peter's arrest and Herod's death (12:1-24), after which Barnabas and Saul's return is described (12:25). The additional detail concerning John Mark (12:12) prepares the reader for the mission to the province of Galatia (13—14).

There are in the letter to the Galatians, however, some additional details which may belong to this visit, sometimes called the famine visit (Gal. 2:1-10; Acts 11:27-29). If the famine visit is described in Galatians 2:1-10, the presence of Titus, a Gentile never mentioned in the book of Acts, is explained. His presence was in the interest of the Gentile mission. The church at Antioch offered a clear example of Gentile conversion; their gift to the church at Jerusalem during the famine offered a clear example of Gentile fellowship. Could other Gentile missions be undertaken with the cooperation of the church at Jerusalem? This visit may have been Barnabas' first opportunity to report to the Jerusalem church the work being done in Antioch.

Does the account in Galatians 2:9-10 relate to Acts 13—14? We do not know. But if it does, then it gives the basis for Antioch's Gentile mission. Such a mission was possible so long as it did not disrupt the fellowship. James, John, and Peter, centering in Jerusalem, would continue their work among the Jews. Barnabas and Saul, centering in Antioch, would go to the Gentiles. They would exercise care to remember the poor at Jerusalem.

John Mark joined Barnabas and Saul in the church at Antioch (12:25). A clear expression of fellowship between Jew and Gentile in the church had developed as a result of Judea's need. Could this fellowship in the gospel continue? How much pressure could it stand?

3. Mission from Antioch (13:1 to 14:28)

If, as seems logical, the visit to Jerusalem for famine relief allowed opportunity for a discussion of a proposed ministry to the Gentile world, the church at Antioch would be quite interested in the conclusions. Any outreach beyond Antioch either must be confined to the Jews or include the Gentiles. The Antioch church favored a mission to include the Gentiles. In what direction should such a mission go?

Chapter 13 begins with a listing of the church's spiritual leadership—"prophets and teachers" (v. 1). Was this the group primarily concerned with the direction of the Antioch church's mission? Little is known of these church leaders. Only Barnabas and Saul are mentioned clearly elsewhere in the New Testament.[6] The fact that Symeon "was called Niger" (13:1) may mark him as a black. Lucius also came from Africa. Of particular interest is Manaen, whose relationship with the Herodian family marks the cosmopolitan nature of the church's leadership. These men, prophets and teachers, heard the Holy Spirit speak while they were ministering and fasting. The call of Barnabas and Saul set the church upon a responsible mission. In praying for and laying hands on them, the church accepted responsibility for their mission. The Antioch church was involved in a new venture with the gospel!

Barnabas and Paul in Cyprus (13:4-13)

Barnabas, a Cyprian Jew (4:36), clearly led Saul and John Mark at the beginning of the mission. That the gospel should be taken to Cyprus was proper, since that was Barnabas' home. For the most part, their preaching was limited to the synagogues. The mission began as a Jewish mission in Gentile territory.

John Mark is described as their "attendant" (v. 5). The word so translated has a meaning beyond that of mere valet, or even assistant. Among its uses in the New Testament is that of a synagogue attendant charged with the responsibility of keeping the scrolls (Luke 4:20). This attendant was a kind of clerk, who also taught in the synagogue school. Teaching consisted primarily of committing to memory passages of Scripture. Certainly, Barnabas and Saul would not need to take such an attendant to the synagogues they visited. John Mark's duties may have consisted of teaching the basic events of the Lord's ministry, and the words of his teaching. If so, he must have recited Christ's teachings repeatedly. As he did so, they became fixed more firmly in his own mind. Tradition holds how useful this rote memory work was to the writing of his Gospel. And then, John Mark was Peter's interpreter. As tradition supposes, much of Simon Peter's personal reminiscences before Christian congregations would have been deposited in Mark's memory.[7]

On the other side of the island, the proconsul, Sergius Paulus, summoned Barnabas and Saul that he might hear the word of God. Since this marked the first appearance of Christian preachers before a Roman ruler, Luke recorded that fact. An adversary appeared in the person of the pseudoprophet Bar-Jesus. Perhaps the proconsul had humored him, and heard his prophecies as a private astrologer. In any event, Bar-Jesus, sensing that the gospel competed with his own teachings, denied its truth. Saul denounced him, even as Simon Peter had denounced Simon the sorcerer. The parallel must have been clear for Luke, who frequently compared the ministry of Peter and Paul.

Before the proconsul of Cyprus the gospel was vindicated by the blindness that fell upon Elymas (vv. 10-12). The Roman official became a believer. All these events made a deep impression upon Saul, whose appointed mission to the Gentiles was beginning to find expression.

Paul and Barnabas in Antioch of Pisidia (13:14-50)

A change in leadership is subtly suggested in the use of the missionaries' names. Verse 9 refers to Saul, "who is also called Paul"—a first use of that name. After his clash with Bar-Jesus, and Sergius Paulus' conversion (vv. 10-12), the account reads, "Now Paul and his company" (v. 13). Clearly Paul had assumed the leader's role. This is the order for the rest of the mission. Since Barnabas was John Mark's uncle, Mark may have been affected adversely by this change. He may have resented Paul's assertiveness. Or, perhaps, John may have sensed the broadening of the mission toward Gentiles and felt uneasy in this new direction for his own ministry. Perhaps he was only homesick. Whatever the case, Paul's disappointment in John Mark's defection was real; so real, in fact, that he refused to take John along on their second mission from Antioch (15:38).

Paul and Barnabas passed from the island of Cyprus to the mainland. Passing through the lowlands of Pamphylia, they pressed toward the higher land in the province of Galatia.[8] They found ample opportunity to preach the gospel in Pisidian Antioch. It was an important city and contained many Jews.

Paul and Barnabas attended synagogue services habitually.
For the synagogue authorities to offer them an opportunity to
speak was quite natural. They were visiting Jews, and appeared
to have something to say. The sermon recorded in 13:16-47 compares favorably with the other sermons recorded in Acts, but also
includes some unique features. For example, Stephen's defense
compared the Messiah to various persons in the Old Testament.
Paul, on the other hand, saw the entire Old Testament as preparation for Jesus. Stephen emphasized Moses as the mediator of
God's revelation, while Paul gave Moses a bare mention. More
space in Paul's sermon is devoted to Jesus, and those events which
marked his ministry, than in Stephen's. In all fairness to Stephen,
it should be added that his sermon was cut short before he planned
to conclude it.

God's historical revelation to his people is as central to Paul's
sermon as it was to Peter's at Pentecost. An emphasis on Israel as
a nation, chosen, created, and educated by God is quite clear.
Canaan became the preparation site for the Messiah's coming, and
David is portrayed as the choice king, anticipating the Messiah's
rule. John the Baptist is presented as the prophetic forerunner.
Jesus, in his passion and resurrection, is the sermon's subject.
Paul directed his hearers' attention especially to the resurrection,
for this was the heart of his experience with Jesus.
The sermon may be simply outlined:

1. God chose our fathers (vv. 16-22).
2. God confirmed his choice in the gift of a Savior (vv. 23-29).
3. God affirmed man's salvation in the resurrection of Jesus (vv.
   30-37).
4. God makes man's salvation dependent on his faith (vv. 38-41).

Although the Jews' response was guarded, they did invite Paul
back on the next sabbath. The following week many Jews talked
with Paul. "Devout proselytes" (v. 43) also talked with Paul.
Some may have brought their Gentile friends, who were on the
verge of accepting Judaism, with them. These proselytes were Gentiles, who, attracted to Judaism's monotheism, ethical standards,
and messianic hopes, had accepted the promises and had been received into Judaism.

On the next sabbath a great crowd gathered. The Jews, moved
by jealousy over Paul's appeal, argued with him and Barnabas.
The gospel's appeal to the God-fearing Gentiles—their own best
prospects for conversion to Judaism—was at the heart of their
jealousy. Paul and Barnabas boldly denounced Jewish selfishness

(vv. 46-47), and appealed to the prophet Isaiah for Old Testament support (see Isa. 49:6). The prophet long before had affirmed God's interest in the Gentile world, an interest which many of the Jews of Paul's day did not share. Where such an interest existed— as in Pisidian Antioch—it appeared suspect. Were the Jews only seeking support for their local synagogue?

With a dramatic statement Paul and Barnabas turned to the Gentiles (v. 46). The Gentiles in Pisidian Antioch were gladdened by the gospel (v. 48). The Old Testament promises, which had seemed attractive except for the legalistic restraints involved, were now offered freely by God's grace. Many believed, and the word spread (v. 49).

Because the required circumcision repelled the men, Judaism had always attracted more Gentile women than men. Women devoted to Judaism were encouraged to use their influence against the Christians. They, along with leading men of the city—who probably preferred a peaceful solution—"stirred up a persecution against Paul and Barnabas, and cast them out of their borders" (v. 50). True to the injunction of Jesus (Matt. 10:14), they simply journeyed to the next city. However, a group of believers was established in the chief city of south Galatia.

Jew and Gentile in Lycaonia (14:1-23)

Despite the turn of events in Antioch, which saw Paul and Barnabas direct their attention to the Gentiles, the missionaries began their work at Iconium in the synagogue (v. 1). The Jews were better prepared for the gospel than the Gentiles, and missionary strategy called for a base of operations in each city. A group of Jewish believers, finding the messianic promises fulfilled in Jesus, provided just such a base in many cities of the Pauline mission. In Iconium, since many Jews and Gentiles believed, the Christian gospel divided the city. Signs and wonders attracted attention; they attested to the truth preached. Probably, Paul and Barnabas were forced out of the synagogue as a result. When violence threatened, they moved to the next city (v. 6).

Paul and Barnabas' ministry at Lystra is unique in the variety of responses given to it. Luke's concise reporting makes missing those responses easy. So, let us look at the story in some detail.

The healing of the Lystran lame man was not unlike that of the Jerusalem lame man under the ministry of Peter and John (3:1-10). Luke's description of this man's condition is quite convincing. In a threefold statement he underscored his lameness: "Impotent in his feet, a cripple from his mother's womb, who never had walked" (v. 8). The physician's description is very definite.

When Paul sensed that the man's faith was strong enough to respond to God's healing grace, he spoke authoritatively, "Stand upright" (v. 10). In contrast to Jerusalem, where the crowd gathered in the Temple area, the gathering place in Lystra was in the city streets. The people shouted acclamation in their native Lycaonian tongue at the man's healing. (Although a part of the province of Galatia, the region maintained something of its ancient identity.) Paul and Barnabas did not at first understand them. Now, as then, language can be a barrier. Those who have lovingly and painstakingly translated the Bible or have interpreted a gospel message can best understand the problem at Lystra.

The crowd's intention can be understood in the light of one of the legends of Lystra. They believed that the Greek gods Zeus and Hermes had visited an elderly couple, Philemon and Baucis. This tale made the miracle very significant, for it seemed clear to the people that Zeus and Hermes had returned. (An interesting confusion of Roman for Greek mythology occurs in the ASV translation: Jupiter is the Roman counterpart for Zeus, and Mercury for Hermes.) What a challenge for the gospel! In a country town two preachers were about to be worshiped because God had healed a lame man who had faith![9]

Paul and Barnabas were horrified when they learned that the people and their priests had mistaken them for gods. And yet, the identification suggests that this was how the people thought gods should act! At least, the situation offered an opportunity for a gospel sermon. The people had been jarred out of the commonplace; they were ready for a simple presentation of the gospel.

As is characteristic with these early sermons, this one fit both the speaker and the situation. The words of Paul portray God as Creator and Sustainer of life (vv. 15-17). Perhaps more time would have allowed Paul to develop the concept of natural revelation in terms of God's specific revelation in Jesus Christ.

Jews from Antioch and Iconium stirred up the crowds against Paul and Barnabas. Frustrated by their inability to worship, and shamed by their misunderstanding of the miracle, the Lystrans were ripe for riot. Some of them felt that they had been deceived; in their anger they stoned Paul. He was made of stern stuff, however. Although bruised and battered, he went on to Derbe the next day.

No details are recorded about Derbe (vv. 20-21), although the area—Derbe and Lystra—is cited as the home of Timothy (16:1). Paul and Barnabas' ministry was fruitful in Derbe (v. 21). For the preachers to have returned through Cilicia, including Tarsus, and back to Antioch in Syria would have been simple. Paul could have continued an earlier ministry in the familiar surroundings of Tarsus. Instead, they retraced their steps through the Galatian cities, strengthening the faith of the new believers. They were interested in the organized life of the churches. They appointed elders (v. 23), who had functions similar to those in Jewish synagogues. (A similar officer may have existed in pagan religious groups.)

Paul had suffered from a physical ailment on his Galatian tour (Gal. 4:13-24). W. M. Ramsay thought of Paul's "thorn . . . in the flesh" (2 Cor. 12:7) as malaria.[10] He had recovered sufficiently by the time of his return to preach in the lowlands of Perga. From there they went to Attalia, and then sailed back to Antioch. Back home at last, they reported on their ministry among the Gentiles.

4. Truth for Today

God uses people according to their gifts. Prominent in the events of this chapter is the contrast between Barnabas and Paul. Yet God used them both. John Mark, different from either of the other men, was used in yet a different way. The truth for us in these men's lives is that God can use each of us. Our varying abilities and experiences complement one another.

Many influences and persons are involved in one person's conversion. Paul's Damascus road experience is a case in point. At first glance, he appears to have come to Christ unassisted. However, examination of the facts discloses several influences: Stephen's life and prayer; the witness of unknown Christians when arrested by Saul; the power of Christ's teaching and life. All had a part in the transformation of Saul the Pharisee to Paul the Christian.

A person may be helped in his Christian life by another's interest. For Barnabas to have rejected Saul as the others were doing would have been easy. However, he believed in Saul's sincerity. Barnabas teaches us that we owe others our interest and trust.

The love of God is not contained. No racial, national, or religious barrier prevents God from extending his grace to men. Should men erect such barriers in a Christian fellowship?

A ministry to the physical needs of others can have spiritual results. Antioch Christians ministered to Jerusalem Christians when they were in want. To talk to a hungry person about the spiritual bread of life without giving him bread for his physical hunger can drive him away from Christ. Meeting physical needs in the name and spirit of Christ often opens the way for spiritual counsel.

We must worship God, not men. Paul and Barnabas were mistaken for pagan gods, and were about to be worshiped. Their example in shunning that worship teaches us to avoid the pitfall of accepting from men or giving to men that which belongs only to God. The witness for Christ must hide himself in Christ.

------

[1] James S. Stewart, *A Man in Christ* (New York: Harper & Brothers, 1935), p. 97.

[2] From *Paul,* by Martin Dibelius. Edited and completed by Werner Georg Kümmel. Published in the U.S.A. by The Westminster Press, 1953. Used by permission.

[3] Political developments may have had something to do with this peace. About this time Emperor Caligula posed a serious threat to Judaism with his avowed intention to set up a statue of himself in the Temple at Jerusalem. From the death of Tiberius in A.D. 37 to the assassination of Caligula in A.D. 41, the Jews had little time or energy to conduct an intensive persecution of the church.

[4] Some manuscripts read "Hellenists" here, instead of "Hellenes" (Greeks). Most modern textual editors have chosen the reading "Hellenes." Preaching to the Grecian Jews (Hellenists) by the Hellenists would hardly have warranted Luke's dramatic description of events in Antioch.

[5] Richard Belward Rackham, *The Acts of the Apostles* (London: Methuen & Co., Ltd., 1939), pp. 169-170.

[6] A "Lucius" is cited in Romans 16:21 as Paul's kinsman.

[7] R.O.P. Taylor, "The Ministry of Mark," in *The Groundwork of the Gospels* (Oxford: Basil Blackwell, 1946), pp. 21-30.

[8] W.M. Ramsay, *St. Paul the Traveller and the Roman Citizen* (London: Hodder and Stoughton, 1895), pp. 94-97, has suggested that the lowlands were bad for Paul's physical condition, and so he had journeyed toward a more healthful area. It is Ramsay who popularized the theory that a malarial condition was Paul's "thorn in the flesh."

[9] *Ibid.,* pp. 114-19. Ramsay offers interesting details about the visit, including some attention to textual differences concerning the location of the intended sacrifice.

[10] *Ibid.,* pp. 94-97.

Freedom at Jerusalem

Acts 11:1-18; 15:1-35

Freedom is won in bits and pieces. For example, our nation's independence will see a two hundredth birthday in 1976. The path to our political freedom has been long and rocky. Where did it begin? at the Boston Tea Party? at Concord? with the struggles of the Baptists in the New World? Or was the beginning at Amsterdam before the sailing from the Old World? or with King John's signing the Magna Charta in A.D. 1215?

In a similar way the mandate of spiritual freedom recorded in Acts 15 has deep roots. Peter and John's ministry among the Samaritans may have been the beginning. Or was it the free offering of the gospel to the Samaritans by Philip? or the impassioned apology of Stephen? Where did the freedom defined in Acts 15 begins?

1. A Preliminary Skirmish (11:1-18)

The credit for freedom does not belong all to one man, even to so great an apostle of freedom as Paul. Peter had reached beyond narrow Jewish lines when he shared the gospel with Cornelius (10:1-48). The Gentile centurion had responded in faith, and received the Holy Spirit and Christian baptism. No heavy burden of legalism had been imposed on his faith, or on the fellowship which he enjoyed with Peter and other Jewish friends. Cornelius' story does not end with Acts 10, however, nor is the impact of the event confined to Caesarea.

A Stern Accusation (11:1-3)
No words were minced upon Peter's return to Jerusalem from Caesarea. The opposing forces spoke clearly and without reser-

Jerusalem: Mt. Zion, center.

vation. Peter had preached to the Gentiles; they had been baptized; word had reached the church in Jerusalem. Peter was challenged by the party of the circumcision. Of course, most, if not all, of the members of the church at Jerusalem were Jewish. However, some Jewish Christians were more strict than others about keeping the Mosaic ceremonial law. These stricter Jews insisted that Jewish rites and regulations be kept within the Christian fellowship; they could not imagine fellowship with non-Jews. The Jews of this rigid sect were called Judaizers.

This circumcision party was a part of the church. Its description appears suddenly in Acts, although it clearly had existed from the first. Indeed, the six men who accompanied Peter to Caesarea are described as men of the circumcision (10:45). They probably were not members of a divisive party, but may have been more legalistic than Peter. Peter and John had been sent by the church in Jerusalem to approve the work among the Samaritans; now Peter himself was suspect because of his visit to the house of Cornelius. This suspicion may reflect the church's thinking, especially after the Hellenists' departure following Stephen's death.

The stated charge (v. 3) was not, however, directed toward Peter's sharing the good news with Cornelius. It was much simpler: Peter was in the house of the Gentile and ate with Gentiles. This was the basic charge. His action offended Jewish Christians who thought Moses' law was to be observed by all. In crossing the barrier to the Gentiles, Peter had erected a barrier between members of the circumcision party and himself.

What is to be done with strong dissension in the church? Does working together in Christ's mission demand absolute agreement? Should certain issues divide a church? If truth is challenged, what then? If love is selective, what then? Both impartial truth and unbiased love should be upheld in the Christian fellowship. This belief was at the core of the conflict at Jerusalem.

A Strong Defense (11:4-17)

Peter's defense was simple. He reported his experience at Joppa in some detail, then all that happened in his visit to Cornelius' house. To compare Peter's account in chapter 11:4-17 to the events recorded in chapter 10:1-48 is an interesting exercise. You will note Peter's emphasis was upon two aspects of the experience: (1) how the Lord dealt with him (vv. 5-10); and (2) how the Spirit dealt with the Gentiles (vv. 11-17).

Peter's spiritual vision, which had preceded the journey to

Caesarea, was intensely personal. The journey, however, was made in the company of six witnesses. The charge against Peter was personal: *"Thou* wentest in to men uncircumcised, and didst eat with them" (v. 3). Peter's defense was established by witnesses: *"We* entered into the man's house" (v. 12).

There was, besides Peter and the six witnesses, a seventh presence: the Holy Spirit. In response to the strong faith in Cornelius' house, the Holy Spirit "fell on them, even as on us at the beginning" (v. 15). There might be long discussion of the rights of Gentiles in the church, but the Holy Spirit had acted to confirm their conversion. Furthermore, he had blessed the fellowship between Jews and Gentiles.

Peter and the Jewish witnesses clearly accepted the sincerity of Cornelius and his friends; the Gentiles were baptized (10:48). The presence of the Holy Spirit, which distinguishes John's baptism from that "in the name of Jesus," was recognized by all. (See 10:48; 11:16.)

Significantly Peter remembered the words of Jesus about the promised Spirit (see 1:5; 11:16). Who could deny the Holy Spirit's work in Caesarea?

Temporary Agreement (11:18)

The translation "they held their peace" (v. 18) suggests that the Judaizers' agreement was given with reservations. The simpler "They became silent" translation is better. When opposition ceased, praise began. The Jerusalem church members accepted what God had done and believed that God was responsible. Simon was not responsible, so there was no point in condemning him. They themselves were not responsible, so there need be no guilt feelings.

Cornelius was treated as the exception. After all, two powerful visions had prepared the way, and the Holy Spirit had come upon him and his household. Members of the church saw and accepted that fact. A question, however, emerged: What would this event do to the image of the church in Jewish society? What sort of social pressures would now be brought on the church because it had included a Gentile household in Christ's mission? Would other Jews withdraw because Cornelius had been accepted? The attitude of nonbelieving Jews toward the apostles would undergo a change, likely. Of interest is the fact that after this episode Herod executed James and arrested Peter (12:1-3).

If the division between nonbelieving and believing Jews became too sharp, how would the resultant pressure affect the mission of

Paul and Barnabas to the Gentiles? Could the circumcision party in Jerusalem stand to be separated from Judaism by the Gentile mission? Where does peace lie in such a situation?

2. The Jerusalem Council (15:1-29)

The heading above usually identifies the Acts material discussed in this section. The heading is justifiable; the Jerusalem Council is among the most significant moments in church history. Luke treated it as critical for the life of the church. That peace came out of so sharp a conflict is surprising. Luke's description does not warrant its being forced into the mold of a modern denominational convention. It was a council arranged to deal with problems which threatened the fellowship of the growing church.

Visitors at Antioch (15:1-3)

The chapter opens with the newer church at Antioch. Only recently the members at Antioch had welcomed Paul and Barnabas back from their highly effective mission among the Gentiles in Galatia. The two church leaders had gone from Antioch with the blessing of the church and had returned to report on their mission. There is no evidence that anyone in the church at Antioch questioned the salvation of the Gentiles by God's grace until "certain men came down from Judaea" (v. 1). Those who questioned are not named.

The bold statement demanding the Gentiles' circumcision was not new. For centuries Judaism had required this rite of any Gentile convert.[1] The stated requirement was directed to the Gentile Christians in the Antioch church. Gentile Christians in Galatia would have been included, but the immediate occasion of conflict was Antioch. The church at Jerusalem disclaimed responsibility for these visitors (15:24), although they represented the position of a group in the church, "the sect of the Pharisees" (15:5). The accusation against Peter by "the circumcision" (11:3) concerned his violation of the Jewish law as they interpreted it. This declaration concerned the salvation of all the Gentiles, and created "no small dissension" (15:2).

The church at Jerusalem had already confirmed the salvation of the Gentiles, both at Caesarea and Antioch. Not all the church, however, had concurred in that confirmation. Paul, Barnabas, and others were directed to go to Jerusalem to discuss the matter with the church leaders there. On their way they reported on their

Galatian mission, and Christians rejoiced at the conversion of the Gentiles.

The Reception at Jerusalem (15:4-7)

The joy of those on the fringe of Judaism—the Phoenicians and Samaritans—is in marked contrast with the distress of those in Jerusalem. Paul and Barnabas reported—perhaps in some detail —on their Gentile missions at Antioch and in Galatia. Moreover, the report was received by the church and its leadership. Certain unnamed Judaizers in the church threw down the gauntlet. The Gentiles must be subject to the law of Moses. "It is necessary" (15:5, RSV).

Paul himself was a Pharisee, but his faith had grown toward maturity through his experience with the Gentiles. He had seen Gentiles turn to Christ, and he himself had turned consciously to the Gentiles. The Judaizers wanted to preserve the best in Judaism, as well as advance Christianity. They might have made choice contributions to the Christian faith, even as Paul did; but they did not. Although they were a part of the Christian fellowship, they could not be permitted to pervert the truth of the gospel.

The issue was drawn sharply. On the one hand were the legalists; on the other, Paul, Barnabas, and Peter. The leaders of the church were summoned to see whether the two positions could be maintained in the same fellowship. It was a good time for a committee to function. When the multitude was excluded, and when it was included, is not altogether clear from the account. The threat to the fellowship was discussed openly. The committee did not file their report away, nor attempt to sweep the whole matter under the rug.

Peter's Speech (15:7-11)

Peter was the appropriate apostle to reply to the Judaizers. His words bear the ring of sincerity, and certainly reflect his own experience. Were the objectors in Acts 15 the same legalists who had complained of Peter's ministry in Caesarea (11:2-3)? His sharing of the gospel with the Gentile Cornelius was well known. If the requirements of the law should be imposed on Gentiles in Antioch and Galatia, they would soon be enforced in Caesarea, too. Peter sensed that freedom was the issue: A person's free response to the gospel, and his free fellowship with all Christians. If there were a threat to freedom anywhere, freedom was threatened everywhere.

Luke's brief explanation is remarkably Pauline and similar to

Paul's defense of freedom made at Antioch (Gal. 2:11-18). Had
Peter discussed the issue with Paul recently? If so, he had learned
from the experience. The law must not become a burden to the
Gentiles as it had become a burden to the Jews (Gal. 5:11). Its
requirements had been overwhelmed by the grace of God in Jesus
Christ, a grace received by both Jew and Gentile. To require compliance with the law was to negate Christ's atoning work. Peter
made his point clearly and forcefully.

Barnabas and Paul Before the Church (15:12-13)
Earlier Paul and Barnabas had reported to the apostles and elders
(v. 4), and perhaps to some persons in the church. As the discussion continued, however, the multitude grew larger. Paul and
Barnabas took advantage of every opportunity to tell of their mission. Barnabas had been Jerusalem's official representative at Antioch, and many were interested in his report. They remembered
his generous gift to the church some years before. His reputation
in the church would command respect. Paul was more independent
of the Jerusalem church; yet many would remember his dramatic conversion. Through the Antioch church's offering both Paul
and Barnabas had ministered to the famine victims in Jerusalem
(11:27-30).

The multitude heard what God had done among the Gentiles.
They were conscious of God's work in their own midst, but were
happy to learn that God worked among folks unlike themselves,
too. The reports silenced the Judaizers. The multitude already was
won to sympathy with the Gentile mission. No argument could
diminish the impact of the reports. The church's leadership had
done their work with sensitivity and insight.

The Chairman's Recommendation (15:13-21)
James seems to have assumed the role of church leader, a fact
that may be implied in Simon Peter's request (12:17) after he
was freed from prison. James was recognized as the leader for at
least two reasons: his physical relationship to Jesus, and his identity with the Jewish position among early Christians. Highly respected among the Jews for his piety and his loyalty to traditions,
he personified their views. Even his reference to Peter as "Symeon"
—the apostle's Jewish name (v. 14)—reflects the circle with which
he was identified. No reference to Paul and Barnabas is made
in James' summary.

James' statement was neatly designed for the situation. The convictions of those who insisted on circumcision for the Gentiles
demanded this speech. They who represented the church's Jewish

roots must not be cut off. James spoke to that audience and its basic needs. However, God had called the Gentiles as his people. James interpreted this development as a fulfillment of prophecy (vv. 16-18). His thought had appeal, doubtless, to the Jewish party members.

James used the Greek translation of Amos (9:11-12)—or else Luke used the Greek in reporting James' remarks. Since the Hebrew version emphasizes the Jews' dominance of all Gentiles —an ancient Jewish dream, James probably quoted the Greek text deliberately. The Greek translation, with its stress on God's universal appeal to all people, was closer to the facts of the Gentile mission. James chose the latter concept, and probably used the Greek version of the Amos passage to support it.

James suggested a compromise with which the reader might take issue. It is important to remember that Paul would interpret that compromise to the Gentiles. James knew this. He felt he could count on Paul's fairness. James' suggestion was twofold: (1) the Gentiles would abstain from idolatry, idolatrous practices, and sexual immorality; (2) they would hold in respect those Jews still faithful to Moses (vv. 19-21). These were the requirements Judaism also imposed on Gentile God-fearers who wished not to submit to circumcision.

Is there anything unfair in the requirement that the Gentiles yield at certain points for the sake of fellowship? The Jews' position had proved flexible. The spirit of the compromise required some giving on both sides. What had the Gentiles to lose in such a compromise? They would observe the law only in its basic moral and spiritual demands. What had the Jewish party members to lose? They would concede God's work among the Gentiles. That was no loss; it was gain.

Notice how closely Jewish Christianity identified with the synagogue. Little wonder that they were at first unsympathetic with the Gentiles' conversion. They had not heard clearly Stephen's call to break ties with tradition. Traditional ties can pose a threat to truth and love. Indeed, certain traditions in today's churches can threaten both the fellowship and the mission of the Christian faith.

Neither James nor the bulk of the church at Jerusalem was willing to deny the conversion of the Gentiles as the Judaizers had done (15:1). Wisely they were concerned about the fellowship, about relations between Jewish and Gentile Christians. How could they relate to one another? It appears from the decision that the Gentiles were expected to respect Jewish traditions. Perhaps it was enough to expect the Jews to accept the report of Gentile conversion.

Report to the Gentiles (15:22-29)

The decision of the Jerusalem Council had to be made known to the Gentiles. Paul and Barnabas were obvious choices to interpret the feelings of the church at Jerusalem. Judas—of whom we know nothing else—and Silas joined them in their visit to Antioch. Later Silas joined Paul on another visit to the Galatians. These men became official messengers from the church at Jerusalem.

The letter was addressed specifically to Antioch, and other parts of Syria, and Cilicia. Neither Cyprus nor Galatia was cited in the correspondence. Yet it certainly was delivered to the cities of Galatia (16:4) by Paul and Silas. The Jerusalem church disclaimed responsibility for the visit by the Judaizers and for the trouble they had caused (v. 24). Certain requirements for fellowship with Jewish Christians were set forth, however, and these the Holy Spirit approved! (15:28). The requirements were minimal; they would be explained by Judas and Silas, whom the church had sent for that purpose. A spirit of charity was expressed in the praise given Paul and Barnabas (15:25-26).

The obvious meaning of the prohibitions in the letter (15:28-29) is that Gentiles must observe certain Jewish food laws for the sake of fellowship. Eating together was a problem because of the idolatrous culture of which the Gentiles were a part. Thus things sacrificed to idols must be rejected. Jews were careful to observe the Mosaic commandments concerning blood. Even today the term *kosher* reflects the long tradition of Jewish food laws. Many Gentiles considered blood a delicacy. The reference to fornication reflects the lax standards of the Gentile world, as well as the practice of prostitution in idol worship.

The decision reflects a kind of minimal morality. The three basic precepts of Judaism were against idolatry, murder, and fornication. An alternate text adds the negative form of the Golden Rule, a fact which tends to suggest the letter referred to simple morality. In any event, these "necessary things" (v. 28) comprise a basic law for the Gentiles in their relationships with the Jews. The inference to draw was that compliance with that law would insure continued good relationships between Christian Jews and Gentiles.

3. Good News at Antioch (15:30-35)

There is no evidence that Paul delivered the Council decision to Corinth and other Gentile churches beyond Galatia. It was made known, however, in Antioch (vv. 30-31); this was the church most immediately involved. The whole church received news of the decision gladly. The words "they rejoiced for the consolation" (v. 31) express the church's satisfaction with the decision. Judas and Silas added personal words to the written decree. The nature of their remarks is suggested by the ASV footnote which reads "comforted" (v. 32).

Interestingly, Judas and Silas are described as prophets, and the church at Antioch was open to the prophetic ministry (11:27; 13:1). Responsiveness to the word and the Spirit of God makes possible knowledge of God's will in a church. Judas returned to Jerusalem, and Silas apparently remained in Antioch.[2] For a while, Paul and Barnabas resumed their ministry there, but soon sensed that God's will for them lay beyond Antioch.

In the background of Luke's account of the solution at Jerusalem is Paul's letter to the Galatians. Clearly, this stirring appeal for Gentile freedom from the Jewish law belongs to the same struggle described by Luke. Scholars do not agree on how these two sources relate to each other.[3] Could the confrontation (Gal. 2: 11-16) of Paul and Peter (with Barnabas also) at Antioch have made the Jerusalem Council necessary? If so, relations were strained severely indeed. The letter to the Galatians may have been written just prior to the events described in Acts 15, making it among the earliest of New Testament writings. Such a stirring call to freedom certainly would have expressed Paul's feelings at this stage, and would have summoned both Barnabas and Peter to Paul's position. The fierceness of Paul's attack on the Judaizers may reflect the sharpness of the discussion at Antioch, and the speed with which they moved into Galatia with their heresy. Is the letter's white heat explained by the conditions of its writing? If Paul wrote it while he and Barnabas journeyed from Antioch to Jerusalem for the Council, then its tone can be understood easily.

The freedom won at Jerusalem was both from old threats and to new possibilities. It meant freedom from the narrow confines of Judaism. It meant freedom from the hindrances the Judaizers would have put on the gospel. It also meant freedom for the church to struggle with its challenging mission. All men now had the chance to respond to an uncluttered gospel: God's good news in Christ Jesus. It meant freedom for fellowship with all men, regardless of national or racial barriers. Indeed, it meant freedom for all men.

The immediate effect of the Council's decision was clear at three points: (1) Its effect on the Antioch church was to encourage a clear declaration of truth. Paul's most effective writing ministry lay ahead, as did the Antioch church's wider mission to the world. (2) Its effect on the Gentiles was to make the gospel more attractive. (3) Its effect on the Jerusalem church was not wholly favorable. Under the leadership of James and others, Jewish Christianity moved in the direction of legalism and traditional Jewish practices. This becomes increasingly clear in Paul's later contacts with the church at Jerusalem, and in the letter of James.

The issue of whether or not Gentiles could be saved apart from the Mosaic law was resolved early in the discussions. Gentiles had received the grace of God in salvation, and their experiences had been confirmed by the Holy Spirit.

The question of fellowship with Jewish Christians was not so easily answered. At this point freedom joins with responsibility in working in Christ's mission in the world. Personal salvation brings one into the body of Christ, which has many members. Working together with those members is often painful. The closer the spiritual ties among the members, the more one is affected by the other. The responsibility one has for the Christian fellowship may appear to limit his personal freedom. However, the experience of an enlarged fellowship generates freedom of a new and larger order.

4. Truth for Today

Sincere demands made upon Christian people can distort the gospel. The Judaizers were sincere people, no doubt. They believed themselves to be right. In contending for Judah's ancient rite as a part of the Christian demand, they were acting according to their convictions.

However, the effect of their efforts was the loss of the profound truth of the gospel. People are saved through repentance from sin and faith in Christ. It is that, plus nothing! Whenever a church, teacher, or preacher implies that salvation is based on Christ plus the meeting of other demands, the pure gospel is lost. Good people, acting from sincere motives, can cloud and distort the simple gospel. As a result, the gospel can be lost.

Christians are expected to live moral lives. In our stress on Christ's complete atoning work, we may not stress enough the effect of his work in a human life. We are not saved by morality, but we are moral after we are saved. The decree of the Jerusalem Council set forth a basic moral standard for worship, social practices, and sexual relationships. The demand of circumcision, so precious to the Jew, was omitted. The demands of the moral law, however, were set out.

The moral demands in the decree were right and practical. They were *right* because "we are his workmanship, created in Christ Jesus for good works, which God afore prepared that we should walk in them" (Eph. 2:10). They were *practical* because the world expects Christians to be a cut above other people in their behavior. The decree included God's purpose and the world's demand.

Christian fellowship can tolerate conflict. We sometimes act as though conflict in a Christian fellowship is to be avoided at all cost. Differences are hushed up; efforts are made to avoid areas of possible controversy.

A lesson from Galatians 2 and Acts 15 is that the open facing of ideas that conflict in a Christian fellowship can be good. In this event a better understanding of the gospel was worked out. Mutual respect between Jewish and Gentile Christians was achieved. The Gentile was reminded, however gently, of Christianity's Jewish roots. The Jew was reminded, however painfully, of Christianity's universal scope. The facing of conflicting ideas in the fellowship became the means for creating a new basis for that fellowship. The new basis made the fellowship broader and stronger.

The Holy Spirit is a unifying presence when conflict occurs among Christians. The open facing of conflict gave the Holy Spirit an opportunity to do his work. Peter reminded his brethren that the Gentiles had heard the gospel from him, under the Spirit's obvious leading. Moreover, the Spirit had fallen upon the Gentiles, and Paul's recounting of the Spirit's power in his work added more light. So much so, in fact, that the Judaizers fell silent.

Do not overlook that silence. For the most part, the Judaizers were not bad people. Nor were they unchristian. They were open

to the Spirit's leading. When they recognized his leadership, they
followed. They ceased to argue. Do you seek to follow the Spirit's
leading when differences occur in your church?

---

[1] Such proselytes were also expected to offer sacrifice in the Temple and
later, at least, to experience the proselyte bath.

[2] Verse 34, which spells this out, does not appear in the best Greek manuscripts.

[3] The churches in Derbe, Lystra, Iconium, and Antioch may be the ones
addressed in the Galatian letter. If so, an earlier date for the Epistle to the
Galatians is possible. If the Galatian mission is that one described in Acts
16:6, the writing of the Galatian epistle had to come after the Jerusalem
Council. The sequence outlined in chapters 1, 2 may be interpreted as relating the Galatians 2:1 visit to Jerusalem with that of Acts 15:2 or Acts
11:29.

A Needy World:
Macedonia

Acts 15:36 to 17:15

M any of the human actions and problems confronting the church today can be found in New Testament times. In Philippi, for example, a demented girl suffered exploitation by greedy owners. A jailer considered suicide because he feared his prisoners had escaped. Civil servants were distressed lest a prisoner make political trouble for them. Crowds in the capital city demonstrated who knows what—their loyalty to Rome? their mistrust of a different faith? their jealousy? Who can tell the real cause of a riot? Troublemakers stirred up misunderstanding, and Christian leaders were forced to leave town. Who would help with such needs? They were personal needs; how could they be met? Could one or two persons do anything helpful?

The story of how Paul and Silas met such needs moves quickly, and in its passing scenes we may find clues on how we can respond to needs today.

1. Sensing the Need (15:36 to 16:10)

Rapid transportation and easy communication have made us aware of our modern world. The television camera can shock a living room group thousands of miles away from the scene of famine or war. How did awareness of world needs come in the first century? Letters, and the visits of persons on the scene stirred such awareness in Paul's day. The Antioch church was known for its world-mission consciousness. Although Paul and Barnabas enjoyed Christian fellowship in that church, and ministered to personal needs of people in Antioch, they looked beyond their city to the world. They remembered the churches in Galatia, and probably had communication with them.

Planning for a Mission (15:36-41)

A return mission tour to Galatia was proposed, and plans were begun. Other members of the church at Antioch must have joined in the plans. There was John Mark, or was he yet at home in Jerusalem? There was Silas, recently returned from the Jerusalem Council. There must have been others. Both Paul and Barnabas were personally committed to a mission beyond Antioch. Both realized the world's need for the gospel. Both had seen what changes the gospel had worked among the Gentiles. Together they made plans to visit "every city wherein we proclaimed the word of the Lord" (v. 36).

There were differences, however, between Paul and Barnabas. Should such differences be allowed to disrupt the deeper agreements? The disagreement over John Mark appears from the first to have been a misunderstanding, and perhaps an expression of unwarranted impatience on Paul's part. More information on Mark's reasons for departure at Pamphylia would be helpful, but we do not have it. Paul must have felt strongly about the subject, and probably expressed himself clearly. The disagreement was sharp. The conflict's sharpness likely was felt more keenly because the fellowship at Antioch was under threat. Boldly Paul had denounced Barnabas and Peter for yielding to the pressure of the Judaizers when they no longer ate with the Gentiles in the church (Gal. 2:13-14). Paul's disagreement with Barnabas over Mark may have poured salt in an open wound.

Barnabas appears to have been more sympathetic with a Jewish mission, and Paul with a Gentile mission. Perhaps John Mark had sided with Barnabas earlier. The question, Was there room for both types of mission? may have resolved the conflict. Of course there was room for both missions in the needy world! And so Barnabas took Mark and sailed for Cyprus, Barnabas' family home, and the scene of an earlier successful mission. Paul chose Silas, a Roman citizen who had experienced the Jerusalem Council, and began a mission through Syria and Cilicia (vv. 40-41). The result was that there were two missions instead of one.

In the spring, perhaps after the Jerusalem Council, Paul and Silas set forth. The weather may well have prevented the passage through the gates of Cilicia before May 1. While Barnabas and Mark set sail to Cyprus, Paul and Silas moved overland through Syria and Cilicia. Their immediate plans were to visit again the churches which Paul had helped establish in Galatia. What other plans challenged Paul?

Choice of Timothy (16:1-5)

Paul had chosen Silas, acceptable to the churches at Jerusalem and Antioch, but another helper was needed. Perhaps because John Mark had proved useful at the outset of the earlier mission, Paul felt that a younger man could be helpful. The mission to Derbe, Lystra, and Iconium had not been a fly-by-night affair. Churches had been established, and ties of friendship had been forged. This was a part of the appeal in a return visit.

On that earlier mission Paul may have led Timothy to Christ. At any rate, he is called a "disciple" (16:1). Paul enlisted Timothy for their mission. Paul considered Timothy's circumcision important (v. 3). He intended to continue going first to the synagogues in new cities, as had been his custom. He did not want Timothy to be an offense.

Later Paul would confess that he had "become all things to all men, that I may by all means save some" (1 Cor. 9:22). In the light of the Council decision, Paul may have appeared to be compromising. Paul, however, was sensitive to the Jews' feelings. Timothy's usefulness on the mission was important. His circumcision appeared best for the mission; that was enough.

The three men made their way through the cities of the previous mission. Luke's interest in how Paul built Christian fellowship may be seen in Luke's mention of the "decrees" from the Jerusalem Council, and Paul's interpretation of them to the Gentile churches (v. 4). Freedom always involves responsibility. The language is Lucan, however; Paul probably would not have referred to the agreement as "decrees." These vital interpretations were a part of the teachings which strengthened the churches. Luke summarized the results of Paul's work (v. 5) before describing the mission's new turn.

Finding God's Will (16:6-10)

The author allows the reader to share in the search for God's will. God's way of giving direction is veiled by the wording. Only the direction is certain. Perhaps a physical condition (malaria?) directed Paul to the northern area, away from Ephesus. Once there, however, they found a sparse population; thus the area was unattractive. Forbidden to speak the word in Asia, prevented from going into Bithynia, the party bypassed Mysia and came to Troas. There had been an impression from the Holy Spirit (v. 6), and a refusal by the Spirit of Jesus (v. 7)—both phrases being ways of speaking about God's direction. Once in Troas, the missioners found no way to go except across the sea. The party might have remained in Troas for a profitable ministry, but God had other plans. Later Paul was to visit the city briefly (20:6-12), but at this point it was only a site in passing.

The sweep and rush of the story is unique; it leads up to the Macedonian vision (v. 9). In the vision is evidence of positive direction. The man of the vision is unidentified, although Luke himself has been named as that man by many. (The "we" passage begins in verse 10.) Apparently Luke enthusiastically joined the mission party as it moved toward a new province. In all likelihood, this was the time of Luke's conversion.

2. Philippi: a Roman Colony (16:11-40)

The description of Philippi as the first city of the district, and as a Roman colony, has led to the guess that it must have been Luke's home city. Thessalonica, the capital of the province of Macedonia, in many ways was more important than Philippi. Philippi was the first city approached on the Egnatian Way after the port town of Neapolis. Philippi was also a Roman colony—a distinction reserved for few places. A colony was established as protection for the empire. When peace came, the legionnaires frequently were granted landholdings, and perhaps citizenship. Their comfortable location in a Roman colony like Philippi strengthened its defenses. Philippi had been the site of two famous battles (42 and 31 B.C.) which helped to set the fate of the empire. Therefore, it was an honored colony city.

As a colony, Philippi was assured a measure of self-government. This fact, along with the provision for land ownership, offered a certain prestige to Philippi. Its civil authorities probably assumed the name "praetors" (translated "magistrates" in v. 20) in imitation of Roman titles. The "lictors" (translated as "sergeants" in v. 35) also were familiar in Roman cities. It was an important city: a Roman colony by Mark Antony's action, and the first city of the region by its own claim. The guess that Philippi was Luke's home is not without reason.

Two sites, Samothrace and Neapolis, were bypassed insofar as Luke is concerned. A favorable wind from Troas made the two-day voyage to Samothrace possible. The trip is described as "a straight course" (v. 11). Later the return voyage took five days (20:6).

Samothrace stood 5,000 feet above sea level and was an imposing island landmark on the sea journey. No evidence of a mission there exists. Neapolis lay approximately 100 miles farther across the sea from Troas. It marked the eastern end of the 378-mile-long Egnatian Way, which crossed Macedonia from east to west. No evidence of a mission in Neapolis has been found.

It is supposed frequently that Paul simply went from place to place, preaching the gospel without any master plan. However, his missionary strategy appears to have been much bolder. He was able to bypass certain areas and cities, even needy places. He wanted to preach in strategic centers. From these centers the gospel could be borne by others to the towns and surrounding countryside. Philippi, a Roman colony, was Paul's first mission center in Macedonia.

A Place of Prayer (16:13-15)
Paul usually went to the synagogue on the sabbath day, but there was no synagogue in Philippi. Ten Jewish family heads were necessary for the establishment and support of a synagogue. Had there been enough Jewish households for a synagogue, the leaders of the Roman colony probably would have frowned on its founding. The authorities would not object, however, to the Jews' gathering for prayer outside the city gates. Paul and his party, supposing this to be true, found the prayer group by the Gangites River. The location on the riverside made possible certain Jewish washings, and, as it proved out, Christian baptism.

Among the women who gathered to worship was Lydia, a businesswoman. She sold purple dyed goods, an expensive commodity, and was of the city of Thyatira in Asia. As head of her house, she seems to have been independent financially. The fact that a woman could engage in business suggests a somewhat liberal attitude in Philippi. Thyatira—Lydia's hometown in Asia—was located in the region of Lydia. Some persons have supposed that she bore the name of her district because she was a former slave.

God opened Lydia's heart to the gospel, and she led her household to accept the good news. Her household probably consisted of servants and employees. Since Lydia insisted that Paul and his party lodge at her house, they made it their headquarters. Thus the stage was set for the generosity which the church at Philippi continually offered the apostle. Paul and his party continued to use the place of prayer by the riverside, and so provoked no conflict. It was a peaceful beginning.

A Demented Girl (16:16-18)
Paul's first problem in Philippi was a slave girl. Her condition is difficult to diagnose from the sparse description. The "spirit of

divination" is literally a "spirit, a python" (v. 16). The Greek god Apollo was symbolized by a python. His shrine at Delphi featured an oracle of great fame.[1] Plutarch referred to ventriloquists as possessing pythons. The girl's calling after Paul has led to the supposition that she was able to throw her voice. This ability, with her demented condition, made her useful to her unprincipled owners. Her fortune-telling would be more attractive with her ability as a ventriloquist. Her condition was not unlike the demon-possessed persons of the Gospels. Paul's presence and preaching would likely have provoked her loud cries, much as the preaching and the presence of Jesus provoked the Gerasene demoniac (Mark 5:1-20). Thus, her healing became important to Paul.

The girl's condition made her proclamation, "These men are servants of the Most High God" (v. 17), unwelcome. The phrase "Most High God" was a Jewish title for God. Greek-speaking Jews and devout Gentiles also used it, although in less orthodox ways. The "way of salvation" had one meaning for the Greek world (v. 17), and quite another for the Christian (see vv. 30-31). For the Greeks the phrase meant deliverance from the powers that govern the fate of man, or the material world. The girl's continued harassment of Paul and his friends became critical.[2] Finally Paul charged the spirit to depart "in the name of Jesus Christ" (v. 18). Immediately the girl was healed.

Arrest and Imprisonment (16:19-24)
The conflict at Philippi was about neither doctrine nor church; it was about money. The slave girl was profitable to her owners; her healing posed for them a loss of income. Both Paul and Silas were dragged before the rulers of the city, where the charge was made. It appears to have been unrelated to the deed (vv. 20-21). However, when an economic problem occurs, the blame often is placed elsewhere. Prejudice against Jews is clear in this incident. The populace rose to the occasion; they accepted the charge made against members of a minority group without any questions. The owners' statement is interesting: "These men, being Jews . . . (we) being Romans" (vv. 20-21). The charge may be summed up: (1) Paul and Silas are causing trouble; (2) they are Jews; (3) they are teaching Philippians to observe new customs—this is proselyting; and (4) they are meddling with us Romans. A part of the charge was the illegal practice of trying to make Christian converts out of Romans.

Again, Claudius' order excluding Jews from the city of Rome because of troubles over one "Chrestus" is in the background. A colony city would be particularly sensitive to its application. The fact of the economic threat, however, is basic. When the release of spiritual power poses a threat to the economic and social structures, opposition will develop. When a pastor seeks to minister to the outcasts in the community, some persons are likely to offer objections. The Christian's course, however, should be laid out, not by the opposition aroused, but by the moral and spiritual values which uphold God's purpose and intention.

In a notable lack of careful investigation, the magistrates ordered Paul and Silas to be beaten by the lictors with rods. This order to scourge the missioners broke the very law which the praetors said they were anxious to uphold. Paul and Silas might have avoided the beating by declaring themselves Roman citizens. However, they may have had no opportunity; the mob action may have come quickly.

The scourged prisoners were entrusted to the jailer and placed in maximum security. The inner prison was probably on a lower level, and their feet were secured by chains fastened between the prison's foundation rocks. Apparently the jailer had an apartment on the upper level, and controlled access to the prison from there.

A Jailer Is Set Free (16:25-34)

Paul and Silas were worshiping in their cell at midnight. The other prisoners were listening to their praying and singing when the earthquake shook the foundations of the prison, and the fetters anchored in the foundation's mortar joints were loosened. The doors, bolted with bars, were shaken open easily.

Most familiar in the story, perhaps, is the question of the jailer, "What must I do to be saved?" (v. 30). No gospel preacher could fail to rise to that occasion! How can there be saving grace for a pagan who has had little or no contact with the Christian gospel? Had he known of the girl's healing "in the name of Jesus Christ"? Had he noticed the calmness with which Paul and Silas bore their beating? Had he understood the prayers the prisoners prayed, the hymns they sang? Was the jailer overwhelmed by the realization that his prisoners had not escaped? It is unlikely that he asked the question about salvation in a mature Christian sense. Paul's reply ignored the jailer's immediate problem and struck at his deepest spiritual need.

Now full freedom came to the locked-in jailer. He found freedom in faith, and with him his household. Before he was baptized, he ministered to the physical needs of Paul and Silas. How quickly the good news of God's salvation spread to all the jailer's house!

The brief statement, "And he was baptized at once, with all his family" (v. 33, RSV) bears no support for infant baptism. Luke's language in verse 34 states clearly that those involved had made personal response to the gospel: "having believed in God." In other words, faith preceded baptism in each instance.

Vindication at Philippi (16:35-40)

The magistrates' second thoughts on Paul and Silas' imprisonment are interesting. The officials decided to free the missioners. The jailer appears to have been happy with the solution and encouraged Paul and Silas to go.

Paul sensed an opportunity and used it. By laws of earlier years, Roman citizens were protected against dishonorable punishment. Paul and Silas, both Roman citizens, had been beaten and imprisoned without investigation. The magistrates immediately recognized the danger of their action. They responded personally; Paul and Silas were set free. Why did Paul react in such a way? Was he getting revenge? Probably his primary reason for asking public release by the authorities was to lift from the Christians in Philippi any taint of illegality. No one could charge them with unlawful assembly, or of following men who broke the law. They left the prison triumphantly, went to the house of Lydia, reported to the other Christians in the city, and departed.

Luke's "we" reference concludes with the imprisonment of Paul and Silas (see vv. 16, 19). Apparently Luke was not thrown in prison, although he had been a witness to the ministry at Philippi. The church there was noted for its generosity to Paul. They sent gifts to him at Thessalonica (Phil. 4:14-16), ministered to his needs in prison (Phil. 2:25; 4:10), and possibly helped again in Corinth (Acts 18:5). Philippi was a victory for the gospel, and remains as a choice church among those established by Paul.

3. Thessalonica: a Roman Capital (17:1-9)

One of the characteristics of Paul's second mission from Antioch was his apparent interest in population centers. Perhaps he interpreted his difficulties in Asia and Bithynia as the Holy Spirit's direction to such centers. In any event, he was not seeking to serve Christ in easy places. Thus on his journey from Philippi he passed through Amphipolis and Apollonia. After traveling almost one hundred miles, he came to Thessalonica. He had traveled the Egnatian Way to the capital city of Macedonia. Here, in a commercial city, with certain civil freedoms guaranteed, he hoped for safety. He also sought an opportunity to influence the surrounding area with the gospel of Christ.

Initial Success (17:1-4)

Since Thessalonica had a synagogue, Paul went there first (vv. 2-3). For three weeks he taught in that synagogue. From the first he spoke boldly and clearly: He concentrated on the details of the Lord's passion, explaining the Scriptures, and comparing texts to demonstrate that Jesus was the Messiah. The sufferings of the Messiah presented a real problem to a Jewish group, and a strong challenge to the Bible teacher. Paul's emphasis was two-fold: (1) the Messiah must suffer; and (2) the Messiah is Jesus. Apart from Jesus' resurrection, the lesson certainly would have been lost on the Jewish hearers. The charge later placed against him (v. 7) suggests that the kingdom of God was also a part of his message.

Both Jews and Gentiles believed. The liberal attitudes of the commercial city made it easy for Jew and Gentile to enjoy Bible study together. Many converts came from the God-fearing Gentiles, among them a number of influential women. These were the best prospects for Judaism, and may have been cultivated for some time by the Jews in Thessalonica. Some who believed probably had enjoyed no previous contact with the synagogue. All those who believed formed a group around Paul and Silas. The gospel they preached removed barriers between Jew and Gentile, and could be accepted much more easily than traditional Judaism.

There is no clear reference to the extent of the Thessalonian ministry. Was there time for a clear break with the synagogue, and intensive work among those who "consorted with" (v. 4) Paul and Silas? At the least, there was time enough in Thessalonica to receive gifts from Philippi (Phil. 4:16), and to establish a church with which Paul would later correspond. Paul and Silas probably spent six months in Thessalonica before the situation became impossible.

A Troubled City (17:5-9)

When the Jews saw the Gentiles whom they had cultivated for their faith following Paul and Silas, they were "moved with jealousy" (v. 5) and incited a riot. There are always those available for such a demonstration; loafers are transformed easily into agitators. The mob's action developed its own momentum (vv. 5-6). Did the rabble take over leadership from the Jews? It was thought that Paul and Silas had taken refuge in Jason's home; thus his house became the object of their assault. When it was clear that they were not there, the mob seized Jason and other Christian friends. They dragged them "before the rulers of the city" (v. 6).

The charge against the Christians in Thessalonica included nothing about religion; it was strictly political. In Philippi, the Jewish community was accused along with Paul. In Thessalonica, however, influential Jews helped keep the Jews from blame. The charge against Paul and his party was couched in the broadest possible terms: "These that have turned the world upside down are come hither" (v. 6). It basically was a political charge, as were those against Jesus (Luke 23:2) and Stephen (Acts 6:11-14). First-century people cherished the peace Rome sought to insure. They opposed any who appeared to threaten it. In Rome, where agitation over one "Chrestus" had caused much unrest, Claudius expelled the Jews from the city. A plea from Paul to the Thessalonians (2 Thess. 3:6-12), written after his ministry there, indicates his sensitivity to the charge that Christians were turning the world upside down. The Thessalonians' charge that Paul and Silas were proclaiming a new emperor was very serious. Later Paul probably avoided an emphasis on the "kingdom of God."

The city's rulers were disturbed at the demonstration and the accusation. Their responsibility was to keep peace when the peace was threatened. Since neither Paul nor Silas was present, a peace bond was the only solution. The politarchs respected their city's favored status, and yet—from their vantage point—they took the mildest action possible. The peace bond, particularly frustrating to Paul, may have been the point of his reference to Satan's hindrance in his letter to Thessalonica (1 Thess. 2:18). He could not resume his work there lest he endanger Jason and his friends. Here, then, were potential legal grounds against the Christian mission. Fortunately the action was purely local, but it does seem to have prevented Paul's return to Thessalonica.

Later Relationships

From 1,2 Thessalonians several additional characteristics of the Thessalonian ministry are apparent. First, persecution was experienced by the entire church (1 Thess. 2:14; 3:3). Second, Thessalonica became a center for the evangelization of the region (1 Thess. 2:14 to 3:10). Third, Paul worked with his hands while there (2 Thess. 3:8). Fourth, he would like to have returned, but Satan hindered him (1 Thess. 2:18). Fifth, some sort of ministry was established, and Paul urged the new church to be an industrious group (1 Thess. 5:12-15; 2 Thess. 3:6-14). Sixth, much of his preaching seems to have been about the second coming (2 Thess. 2:1-12).

Paul's need to make an abrupt departure from Thessalonica was disappointing to him. Did Paul hover nearby at Beroea, hoping for a chance to return? Timothy appears to have remained in Thessalonica, for verse 10 mentions only Paul and Silas. Later, both Silas and Timothy were left in Beroea while Paul went to Athens alone (v. 14). Thessalonica, the Roman capital of Macedonia which had been attractive in prospect, proved a disappointing experience. Yet, despite the trouble, a church was established in that city.

4. Beroea: A Brief Ministry (17:10-15)

Just off the Egnatian Way, about sixty miles from Thessalonica, lay Beroea, the center of a prosperous farming district. Probably not in Paul's original plans, it became a refuge from the difficulty at the capital city. Paul and Silas began their Beroean ministry in the Jewish synagogue.

Initial Success (17:10-12)

The brief description of the Beroeans as "more noble" (v. 11) and "examining the Scriptures daily" (v. 11) is familiar to all students of Paul's mission. The Beroeans heard Paul and Silas gladly, and opened their minds to the truth. The understanding was sharpened by their interest in the Scriptures. They did not accept right off everything they heard, but checked the missionaries' teaching by the Scriptures. This was their nobility: their readiness of mind. Mentally alert and spiritually hungry, many responded to the gospel message. Among them were influential Greek women who found in the Christian gospel the spiritual truth they had sought. No separation from the synagogue was necessary at Beroea, although the influence of Paul and Silas appears to have spread beyond the synagogue. Later one of the church members, Sopater, accompanied Paul to Jerusalem (20:4).

Trouble and Departure (17:13-15)

The ministry at Beroea was successful and peaceful until the troublemakers at Thessalonica learned that Paul was nearby. They were determined to rid themselves of this threat. Paul's trouble did not begin with the governmental authorities in either Thessalonica or Beroea, and does not appear to have been widespread in the province. He departed Beroea at the first sign of trouble, lest another adverse decision make his return to Thessalonica more difficult. His friends were anxious, as they had been at Thessalonica, to protect him. They rushed him to the sea. Was this plan designed to conceal Paul's real destination—Athens? A refreshing couplet which dates from the third century B.C. goes: "He who fights and runs away lives to fight another day." Paul's effectiveness was preserved for later ministry.

Paul's distribution of his missionary forces at his departure from Macedonia suggests a degree of planning and organization on his part. He went to Athens, perhaps again in a sort of holding operation, hoping to return to Thessalonica. Silas and Timothy remained in Beroea. They may have remained to await news permitting his return. Timothy visited Paul at Athens, and was sent back to Thessalonica (1 Thess. 3:1-2). Perhaps Silas also came to him there and returned to Macedonia. Later (18:5) both were welcomed by Paul at Corinth.

Thus Paul's work in Macedonia ended on a tentative note. Paul had gone to Macedonia in response to a divine call. He had established churches in Philippi and Thessalonica, churches with which he later corresponded. Opposition to his mission had come from Gentile businessmen as well as Jews. The resentment of the Jews at the ease with which he attracted prospective Gentile converts was certain to affect relationships between Paul and Jerusalem. Must the needy world wait for the resentment to recede?

5. Truth for Today

God uses committed people to get his work done in the world. Clearly the world's needs could not be satisfied by Paul's small force, but his work provides a clear example of what a very few can do. To be sure, the churches at Antioch and Jerusalem were involved in the mission, and their support meant much to Paul. However, there is no evidence that this support was financial or physical; only moral and spiritual. Yet, Paul maintained a continuing respect for and response to these churches. They all worked together in Christ's mission.

Paul used every opportunity. His initial approach was made to the Jews. The gospel was not, however, confirmed to them, nor even to those Gentiles who had been attracted to Judaism. Paul used that opportunity to open other doors. Churches today find some doors closed to their members. Witnessing is not always easy. Church leaders must be as alert as Paul was; they must help create witness opportunities for their members. Christians must be as sensitive as Paul was; they must make Christ's gospel clear in the world where they work and live. Paul did not wait for people to come to him; he went to them.

Disagreement between church leaders is possible. However, God can and does bring something good out of such disagreements. Two men, committed to God's will, may interpret that will differently; but because of their personal commitment, they earnestly will seek to serve God.

Older Christians need to encourage and help the young. Likely no one would have heard of Timothy had it not been for the encouragement given him by Paul and Silas.

God's will is not always easy to know. Sometimes our own plans or ideas get in the way. However, God does lead his children when they seek his way. For Paul, it was a day-to-day, city-by-city following of God's leadership. On occasion, a likely opportunity must be by-passed.

When Christian action challenges self-interest, conflict may come. In Lystra, Paul was opposed because he uncovered the Lystrans' false worship. In Philippi, conflict came from persons threatened by loss of income. In Thessalonica, the cause for opposition was religious pride. Selfishness and greed are gods which many serve, even some persons who are members of churches.

What a blessing for God's people to study the Scriptures! Where there is great interest in God's Word, and a will to know its truths, the people grow in spiritual depth; the pastor's ministry is pleasant and effective. The memorial to the Bereans is a lasting tribute: They searched the Scriptures daily to see "whether these things were so" (17:11).

---

[1] The chief agent at Delphi was a virtuous woman who, drugged to some degree, spoke and then was interpreted by nearby priests. Apollo was thought to have the power of communicating this gift of oracle-speaking to others besides the Pythia at Delphi. Such a one was the female slave at Philippi, "probably a ventriloquist, afflicted with lunacy of a mild chronic type, whose peculiarity was, according to the ideas of the time, looked upon as caused by her being possessed with a Pythonic spirit." She was consulted by her "master and mistress, rather than a group of men." Her owner interpreted her cries, in the manner of the priests at Delphi, and framed out of her cries answers to those who consulted her. See P.A. Gordon Clark, "Python," *Dictionary of the Apostolic Church,* ed. by James Hastings (Edinburgh: T. & T. Clark, 1919), pp. 292-93.

[2] The reference to "many days" (v. 18) indicates that the ministry at Philippi extended for some time before the imprisonment.

Challenging Cities:
Athens and Corinth

Acts 17:16 to 18:17

Each of the cities of the Mediterranean area has its own popular religious center. Thus, Jerusalem has its ancient Temple site; Rome its St. Peter's Cathedral. Overlooking and overwhelming Athens is the Acropolis, with its Parthenon. The site of ancient Corinth, too, is overwhelmed by the majesty of its Acro-Corinthus. Jerusalem and Rome belong to the Judeo-Christian tradition. Athens and Corinth reflect the pagan culture and religion of ancient Greece. Paul confronted the paganism of these latter Gentile cities with the gospel of Jesus Christ.

Besides the challenge of entrenched paganism, there was the striking contrast between the culture of Lystra, for example, and the culture of Athens. When Timothy, a native of Lycaonia, visited Paul at Athens (1 Thess. 3:1-2), he must have seen that contrast most clearly. Paul, a native of Tarsus—"no mean city" (Acts 21:39)—obviously sensed the challenge in Athens and Corinth. Athens was the cultural and intellectual center of the world. Students from everywhere were attracted to it and walked its streets, seeking fresh knowledge. Corinth was a significant commercial center, and people came there to seek gain. Athens and Corinth were as different as night and day.

Twentieth-century America is fast becoming a nation under the influence of its cities. The gospel has not changed, but the environment in which it is communicated has been altered radically. Many Americans have moved from the quiet countryside to the bustling city. The challenge of the rural church with its power to influence a community is attractive, but the modern American cities—Athens or Corinth of old—pose their challenge, too.

Before Paul arrived in Athens, he and his party had lived in

The Acropolis of Athens.

status-conscious Philippi. After that it was Thessalonica, whose
political power offered an appealing challenge. The political power
of Thessalonica, however, halted the missionaries' efforts. Now
Paul was in Athens, a city devoted to pagan religions and culture.
Luke's report sets the spine tingling: "But they that conducted
Paul brought him as far as Athens" (v. 15).

1. Athens: A Very Religious City (17:16-34)

Our heading was Paul's description of Athens (17:22), and the
account confirms that description as accurate. However, Athens
was not Christian, or Jewish, but was noted, rather, for its many
religions. The evidence was the wide variety of altars to pagan
gods erected there. The Athenians maintained many religious
shrines. They worshiped at them all, but found none really
satisfying. To confront such burned-out religionists was difficult.
Little wonder that Paul waited quietly for a few days, hoping for
Timothy and Silas to bring good news from Thessalonica.
Initial Ministry (17:16-17)
Paul was not quiet long, however. His preaching in Athens was in
reaction to the city's idolatry (v. 16). The city was "full of idols";
each one of them challenged him. There were idols along the
street, and idols in the markets. The Acropolis, with its Parthenon,
Temple to Victory, and Temple of Erechtheus—all architectural
masterpieces—moved Paul to action.

For viewing the Acropolis, Paul might have sought the Hill of
the Muses, itself a part of the ancient Athenian's interest in
religion and culture. These muses inspired the art, architecture,
music, and drama, all of which centered in pagan religious events
or deities. Athens traditionally had combined its culture and
idolatry so that the one reinforced the other.

In the past certain cities in America have identified religion with
culture in such a way that persons of other religious views or
from other cultures were quite uncomfortable. However, this
kind of setting is fast passing from the American scene. Rather,
Christianity must now contend with many religions, sects, and
even superstitions. The witnessing task today is challenging, but
no more so than that which faced Paul.

Paul began his ministry in the Jewish synagogue. Luke presents
a strange flow of ideas: Paul was provoked by the idols, so he
reasoned with the Jews and the God-fearers in the synagogue
(v. 17)! (There were God-fearers among the Gentiles in Athens,

as there had been in other cities of Paul's mission.) They, and the Jews, must have shared Paul's discomfort with the pagan idols. The synagogue gave Paul a base of operations, and placed him in a familiar setting.

Paul's ministry extended beyond the synagogue, however, for he was interested in the persons who made up the city. Some of these persons crowded daily in the marketplace (agora), and there Paul met them. The agora was the scene of brisk trading, of news as well as wares. This wide place, surrounded by public buildings, porticoes, and shops, attracted the curious as well as the traders. Soapbox orators of a modern Hyde Park or Central Park would have been at home in the agora. In ancient Athens, Socrates had claimed the agora as his arena. Now, in the agora, Paul challenged all comers with the gospel.

Encounter with Philosophers (17:18-21)

Among those who met and talked with Paul were the Epicureans and the Stoics, representatives of two popular philosophies of the time. They, too, walked the streets of Athens, seeking to win followers. Indeed, Paul himself might well have passed for one of these walking philosophers of that ancient city. To some degree, these thinkers had replaced the idols and their priests. Understanding them [1] helps us understand ancient Athens.

The Epicureans are usually charged with the pursuit of pleasure, and this is a just charge. Their wisdom was disclosed, however, in their choice of those pleasures which they pursued. They sought those pleasures which give long-range satisfaction. Long since they had given up devotion to or dependence upon the gods of ancient Greece. They believed them to be utterly unconcerned about human affairs. They were materialistic in their outlook, however, and did not accept the concept of life after death. Perhaps this philosophy gave rise to Paul's statement, "If the dead are not raised, let us eat and drink, for tomorrow we die" (1 Cor. 15:32).

The Stoics were a nobler lot, and claimed a porch (*stoa*) on the agora as the site of Zeno's teaching. They named themselves after their master's teaching place. While there may be some modern Christians who show evidence of kinship with the Epicureans, there are others whose Christian faith is similar to stoicism in some aspects of its outlook. The followers of Zeno were a sternly self-disciplined group, and resisted the claims of human passions and desires. They believed God to be a spirit dwelling in all parts of the creation. They considered life to be ruled by fate rather than faith. They bore the stings of circumstance with dignity, although a strong tendency to suicide marked them. To the Stoics all men were brothers, for all partook of the divine spirit which pervaded creation.

Professor Keck suggests three elements of the stoic philosophy: (1) "The Stoics believed that the universe (and everything in it) was ruled by Law" (Logos). (2) "Man lives in a closed world, a world of cause and effect." Hence, they thought "man ought to accept his destiny." (3) "Man does, however, find himself driven by passions and bound by ignorance and custom." Therefore, the Stoics appealed to men to "abandon such a life, to live reasonably, to live according to the Logos, the Law of the universe." [2] Like the Epicureans, the Stoics rejected any hope of a future life, convinced that this one was bad enough.

In all probability there were other beliefs represented in the agora that day, for Athens was a melting pot of the world's ideas. Response to Paul's teaching was varied. Since the Athenians were accustomed to strange teachings, some described Paul as a "babbler" (v. 18), who picked up ideas here and there and spouted them forth. Others, conversant with the idolatry of the city, interpreted his teaching in terms of new deities. Paul did speak of Jesus and his resurrection. Both words were unfamiliar to the Athenians. Since in their language "Jesus" was a masculine word, and "resurrection" was a feminine word, some who heard Paul thought he was teaching about a new pair of gods. Little in their religious ideas prepared them for any concept of personal life after death.

To protect the reputation of the city as an intellectual center—frequented by students from all over the world—the city officials subjected Paul to investigation. He was led to the Areopagus for further inquiry. The site of the questioning is perhaps the Hill of Ares (a literal translation of Areopagus), which is near the agora. It is known today as Mars' (the Roman name for Ares) Hill. On the other hand, the Areopagus may refer to the name of the court before which Paul testified; it may have met in the agora itself. Luke's judgment of the city's fickleness indicates a lack of sympathy for Athens: they spent their time moving about from idea to idea. To them, the Christian message was simply a new idea—one among many.

"In the midst of the Areopagus" (17:22-31)

How should Paul begin his apology for the Christian faith in so distinguished a company? What would a modern preacher say? Most of those travelers who ascend to the hilltop where Paul is supposed to have stood are content merely to reread Paul's sermon. He might have begun logically by appealing to the Stoics and declaring, "The Logos became a human being and walked on earth with us" (see John 1:14). Such a statement would not likely have shocked them. However, since Paul had been charged with presenting new gods, he began, not with a philosophical idea, but with a statement that fit their idolatrous background. His logic is clear.

Idols in Athens had been made to represent a wide variety of human experience. From Mars' Hill Paul could look down easily on the agora, and over to the Acropolis with its temples, altars, and idols. On the Acropolis stood an altar to Mercy, and a temple to Victory. Paul had sensed a longing for the true faith in another altar, "To An Unknown God" (v. 23). Beginning there, Paul witnessed to the Athenians. Perhaps the title of his sermon that day would have read, "To An Unknown God." The God whom Paul preached was largely unknown to the Athenians.

A frequent translation of the description, "Ye are very religious," is, "Ye are too superstitious" (v. 22). This latter translation likely would have been rejected by the Athenians. The description "very religious" is accurate, and could apply to the modern scene, as well as to Athens. Paul began where the Athenians were, and proceeded to preach in terms they could understand. At the same time, he was laying the groundwork for a gospel appeal. That appeal may be found in verses 30-31. It is a word on judgment, and man's need to repent.

Compared with other sermons in Acts, this presentation of the good news appears strange. It does, however, reflect the context of Athens. Its ideas would appeal to the Stoics who heard Paul. That he showed understanding of pagan ideas is not, however, to say that Paul accepted them. Compare, for example, this passage with Romans 1:18-32. Both passages reflect an understanding of natural theology; neither is confined in its subject matter to God's revelation in Judaism.

Paul's Mars' Hill sermon may be outlined as follows:
1. You know many gods (vv. 22-23)
2. I present to you *the* God (vv. 24-29)
    (1) He is creator of all things (vv. 24-25)
    (2) He is sovereign and sufficient (v. 26)
    (3) He made men
        all men, that they should seek him and find him, for he is near (vv. 27-28)
    (4) He is Spirit (v. 29)

3. You are to repent (vv. 30-31)
   (1) God commands it (v. 30)
   (2) God will judge the world (v. 31)
       in righteousness
       by a man whom he raised from the dead (v. 31).

Although the sermon was phrased partially in stoic language,[3] it broke sharply with stoic views. Rather, Paul insisted on a particular revelation of God in Christ. He refused the concept that all religions are good, and all will eventually lead to God. As for the Athenians, neither the judgment nor the resurrection was acceptable. The former upset the peaceful order which the Stoics accepted, and the latter extended life beyond death.

Division of Opinion (17:32-34)

The crowd understood well enough to respond. Paul had spoken clearly to them. They were curious about Paul's reference to Jesus and the resurrection, but they were shocked when he went on to say that God raised Jesus from the dead. They could talk about the abstract idea of immortality; they rejected the idea of personal resurrection. "Some mocked," but others were still curious and wanted to hear more (v. 32).

Since Paul realized better than they their distance from Christian commitment, he departed. The establishment of a church in Athens is not reported at this time, for the implication is clear that only a few Athenians believed. Among those who followed him were Dionysius and Damaris (v. 34). The more prominent was Dionysius, who was a member of the supreme tribunal that met on the Hill of Ares (Areopagus [v. 34]). Tradition identifies Dionysius as the first bishop of Athens. The very mention of the names Dionysius and Damaris implies that their names were known to Christians of the area at the time Luke wrote.

Of great interest to us is the mood in which Paul now approached Corinth. The mission to Athens was less than a striking success, and Paul had for the first time met Greek culture head-on. Could the Christian message make an impact on the pagan world? Paul had been frustrated by the closed door at Thessalonica. Now Athens had mocked his message, with few to respond. What lay ahead in Corinth?

2. Corinth: A Responsive City (18:1-17)

Although Athens easily outranks Corinth in the modern mind, first-century citizens found the two about equal in importance.

The distance between them was not great, perhaps fifty miles. The difference between them, however, was immense. Whereas Athens was a center for learning, Corinth was a center for commerce. Before the New Testament period, the towering Acrocorinth (approximately 1800 feet above the plain's floor) was a vantage point for the control of the sea. When the Romans guaranteed the peace, and Julius Caesar built the colony city, its location on the narrow isthmus between the Aegean and Adriatic Seas assured a commercial character. (The ancient dream of a canal across the isthmus, which connected the mainland with the Peloponnesus, was realized only in the modern period. Now the canal's sleek sides and stunning depth boggle the imagination: What might Corinth have been in the ancient world with this canal?) The shorter route from Asia to Rome was across the isthmus. Small boats were simply hauled overland from Cenchreae to Lechaeum, which were Corinthian ports on opposite sides of the isthmus. Larger vessels were unloaded at one port; the cargo moved overland, and then reloaded on another vessel at the other port.

Corinth's access to the sea, and its importance to transport in the Roman Empire insured its significance and size. The constant movement of ancient mariners also insured its sin. The reputation of Corinth was so bad that the phrase "to Corinthianize" meant "to make immoral." Its Roman freedom was abused; its devotion to Greek idols became the occasion for sexual gratification. Its spiritual needs were great. Paul, fresh from his frustration in Athens, was challenged.

The modern Christian can find more in the New Testament about church life in Corinth than in any other city. Paul ministered there for at least a year and a half. From that city he probably wrote 1,2 Thessalonians, and Romans. Paul wrote several letters to Corinth, two of which have been preserved. They are thought by many New Testament students actually to represent four letters from Paul. It is from these letters, for example, that we sense the spirit in which Paul moved from the natural theology of Athens to the Christ-centered theology of Corinth: "And I, brethren, when I came unto you, came not with excellency of speech or of wisdom, proclaiming to you the testimony of God. For I determined not to know anything among you, save Jesus Christ, and him crucified" (1 Cor. 2:1-2).

Aquila and Priscilla (18:1-3)
Silas and Timothy had been left behind at Thessalonica; thus the apostle arrived in Corinth alone. Soon he discovered a couple

who developed into close friends, Aquila, a Jew from Pontus, and his wife, Priscilla. The majority of the New Testament references list Priscilla first, a mark of her influence as a Christian in her own right. (See Acts 18:18,26; Rom. 16:3; 2 Tim. 4:19.) They were destined to be remembered because of their involvement with Paul and his mission.

Had Paul known them previously? Apparently they were Christians before this encounter. Already the gospel had reached Rome. The presence of Aquila and Priscilla in Corinth, so recently come from Rome, may have sparked the apostle's interest in the capital of the empire. The second-century writer Suetonius relates that in Rome the Jews had disagreed so violently over a person named Chrestus that synagogue life was disrupted. Even the peace of the city was threatened. The modern reader readily can see in *Chrestus* a misspelling of the Latin *Christus*. Was the Jewish community split over its messianic hopes? If so, we can guess that the cause of this division likely was the preaching of the gospel of Jesus Christ. Synagogues, as we have seen, were split often by the gospel's proclamation. In any event, Emperor Claudius issued a decree that all Jews leave the city—a sizable exodus. Among those who departed were Aquila and Priscilla (18:2).

They were tentmakers by trade, and so was Paul. All Jewish boys were taught a trade; even the rabbis worked with their hands. The tents of Paul's youthful labors were made of Cilician goat hair, which was tough and fibrous. He was an experienced workman, and found this additional tie with the Christian couple a natural one. Indeed, he later took pride in his independence of his Corinthian converts; he was not a burden to them. (See 1 Cor. 9:8-18.)

A Change in Pace (18:4-5)
Paul's initial ministry was greatly restrained, for he worked with his hands during the week and argued in the synagogue only on the sabbath. Corinth was not noted for its walking philosophers, and its agora was busier with trading than with talk. There were, to be sure, Greeks who had been attracted to the synagogue, and Paul sensed their need for the gospel.

Then Silas and Timothy came down from Macedonia (v. 5). The change in Paul's ministry was immediate. His weekly discussions at the synagogue were transformed into powerful preaching services. Luke described the new mood as "constrained by the word" (v. 5). It was as though Paul had removed his self-imposed restraints; his only thought was to make the gospel clear. His tongue was freed, and he became a much more effective witness. Before the arrival of Silas and Timothy, he "reasoned" (v. 4), perhaps, in the pattern he had used in Athens. After their arrival, "Paul was constrained by the word, testifying to the Jews that Jesus was the Christ" (v. 5). The change is obvious.

Why should the arrival of friends from Macedonia make this great difference? Paul's concern for the work in Thessalonica had overshadowed his work at both Beroea and Athens. However, when his friends arrived with their news from Thessalonica, the burden of anxiety was lifted. Paul was free to preach. A reference to such a visit in Paul's letter to Thessalonica (1 Thess. 3:6-10) suggests that the news from Thessalonica was good. The church at Philippi may have sent a gift (see Phil. 4:10-16). If so, this would have freed Paul from dependence on his tentmaking. He carefully preserved his financial independence from the field where he worked, but received help from churches which he had established previously. With a new sense of vigor, Paul worked at the mission on which he had set out from Antioch many months before. Paul's friends, Silas and Timothy, reminded him of his relationship with the churches of Antioch and Lystra. Jerusalem was represented in Silas (see Acts 15:27,32,40), and thus shared in the mission. Paul was encouraged in the work, and proceeded at a quickened pace.

To the Gentiles (18:6-8)

Paul's change became apparent to the Jews in Corinth. Relationships had been peaceful in the synagogue, but Paul's preaching took on new power. Some of the Jews were driven to blasphemy by their rejection of Jesus. They recognized in Paul a threat to their traditional faith. Opposition was organized, and the break became inevitable. In a dramatic scene, Paul "shook out his raiment" (v. 6) and announced his turning to the Gentiles. The Jews rejected Paul, and he turned to the Gentiles. The synagogue could no longer hold the rapidly rising leaven of the gospel.

The house of Titus Justus was next door to the synagogue. After Paul declared himself sent to the Gentiles, he went to Justus' home. Titus Justus was a Gentile God-fearer who had become convinced that Jesus was the Messiah. Unfortunately for the synagogue, many of their best prospects believed the gospel and were baptized (v. 8). The Jews' loss of Crispus, ruler of the synagogue, was a heavy blow, and made relationships with the synagogue Jews more difficult. Paul does not appear to have been concerned about the break; instead, he earnestly sought to witness to Corinthians of every race and belief. As a result many were baptized (v. 8). Although the church was composed mostly of Gentiles, some Jews—such as Crispus (v. 8)—were in the church.

An interesting note in 1 Corinthians 1:14-16 concerns Paul's baptizing of converts. In a rebuke to Corinthian Christians who were jealous over religious leaders, Paul referred to his baptizing Crispus and Gaius. Also, Paul remembered he had baptized his first Corinthian convert, Stephanas (1 Cor. 1:16). Beyond these persons named, Paul wrote, "I baptized none of you." Likely, Silas and Timothy's coming relieved Paul of the need to baptize persons himself.

A Reassuring Vision (18:9-11)

Rejected by the Jews, and separated from the synagogue, Paul and his friends were now exposed to the Gentile world. Perhaps the success of the ministry at Corinth proved embarrassing and dangerous. Having established the work, should he leave the city before trouble came? Would it be wise to risk another peace-bond situation? That would mean danger for new Christians. The Jews' opposition in the nearby synagogue was a continuing problem; Paul must have struggled for clear direction.

Paul was given assurance through a vision (vv. 9-10). Had he thought of going back to Thessalonica to give them needed nurture? (See 1 Thess. 3:10.) Whatever the case, the Lord spoke to Paul as clearly as in the Macedonian vision at Troas. His directions were as follows: (1) Stay here and speak boldly (v. 9); (2) I am with you (v. 10); (3) no harm shall come to you (v. 10); (4) I have claimed Corinth for my own (v. 10). Paul was convinced by the vision; he remained in Corinth for a year and a half. This appears to be his longest stay in one place until Ephesus.

Acts offers no details on this extended ministry except to indicate that Paul was "teaching the word of God" (v. 11). Does this statement indicate that converts were coming so freely to the house of Titus Justus that Paul's work was primarily that of teaching? The brief statement made in verse 11 may mark the Corinthian ministry as one similar to that at Syrian Antioch where Barnabas and Saul "taught much people" (11:26). Was Corinth intended to be the Antioch of the West?

Corinth did become the center for Achaia. The details offered by the Corinthian letters suggest that Paul and his friends established a strong church there. Persecution did not appear to be a problem, and the membership was free to develop their spiritual gifts. The names of Christians cited in the letters suggest the intensive work done during this period. Organizational problems did not concern Luke, however. He was more interested in the establishment of the church and the defense of the Christian faith in the light of Roman law.

Trial Before Gallio (18:12-17)

Little in the Acts account helps us date events. The first three chapters of the Gospel of Luke, on the other hand, offer details about rulers and historical events. The mention of Gallio in 18: 12 is one of few such details in Acts. His coming to Corinth as proconsul offers a possible date on which a chronology may be based.[4] This reference, however, is not conclusive. We can only guess that when Gallio became proconsul in A.D. 51-52, the Jews likely would take advantage of his presumed inexperience to make their legal attack on Paul.

Paul had enjoyed a prolonged and peaceful ministry in Corinth. When Gallio came there, the Jews united to drag Paul before the judgment seat where the new tribune sat. Acts suggests that all the Jews in Corinth moved against Paul at one time. Their patience was exhausted by his preaching, and they decided that a charge must be made before a Roman governor. Their desperation marks the success of the Christian mission. The Jewish leaders in Jerusalem had gained the sympathy of Pilate in an earlier day, but Gallio was not fooled by their charges of unlawful acts (v. 13). The charge is similar to that made at Philippi (16:21), although there it was made by Gentiles, not Jews. It was a religious charge, not a political one. The Jews likely would not dare to make a political charge against anyone. The increasing tension between Jew and Roman would prohibit that.

Judaism was a legal religion, and enjoyed certain rights under Roman law. Extensive proselyting among Romans was frowned upon, but the Jews were relatively free of Roman interference in their religious activities. The Jews' strategy appears to have been to get a clear separation of Judaism and Christianity. Thus exposed as non-Jewish, Christianity might have been judged an illegal religion.

Paul was about to offer his defense before Gallio when the judge spoke up. From the statement made by Gallio, it appears that he had had previous experience with such Jewish charges. He was annoyed by the prospect of a religious quarrel, and refused to make a judgment. A degree of vindication for Christianity can be found in his dismissal of the charges. However, the encounter, which might have produced dialogue between Paul and Gallio, was nonproductive because of Gallio's indifference. The ruler of the synagogue—Sosthenes—was nearby, and bore the brunt of the Jews' frustration. He was beaten for the trouble he had caused. Again, Gallio did not interfere. It is intriguing to note that a Sosthenes is cited in 1 Corinthians 1:1 as Paul's brother, and that Paul wrote from Ephesus (1 Cor. 16:8).

3. Truth for Today

Christian truth is both profound and simple. It has an appeal to the learned and unlearned. Our task is to become effective witnesses to all men of whatever station. We must learn to apply Christian truth to life in whatever state we find it.

God's love extends to all. Two converts are named at Athens: Dionysius the Areopagite, and "a woman named Damaris" (17: 34). Which one of these would receive more attention on joining a church today?

The number of converts may not be a valid measure of effectiveness. We should not judge Paul's effectiveness in Athens by the few converts he won there. Paul contended with many factors on Mars' Hill. He did win converts; tradition holds those converts established a church. We know that Athens today is a stronghold of Greek Orthodox Christianity. Corinth, where Paul had many converts, is not nearly so significant today.

A pastor needs the support of concerned friends to make his ministry fully effective. Paul was far more effective in Corinth after Silas and Timothy joined him there. They gave him needed spiritual and emotional support; they assisted him, likely, with matters such as the baptism of new converts.

A pastor may bog down in details of worthy church work, and have little time or energy left for the ministry of preaching, teaching, and care of souls. Church members can help him by taking responsibility for the church's financial needs and the details of church work. This is working together.

Christian truth can be divisive. When Christian truth is presented and understood clearly, it separates those who accept it from those who reject it. The Jews in Corinth recognized the conflict between their interpretation of the Jewish tradition and Paul's interpretation of its fulfillment in Christ. A principal difficulty of the church today is the refusal of some of its members to make the needed break between culture and the demands of Christian truth.

God is concerned about the city. Its decision makers often challenge his truth. Its influence extends far beyond its borders. Its materialism denies spiritual reality. Its moral values challenge God's moral standards. Its culture challenges his church. Therefore God has set his people in the cities, as well as the towns and the open country.

---

[1] It will probably be helpful to read an article on these two philosophies. A Bible dictionary, or an encyclopedia, will outline their beliefs. Most commentaries on Acts will offer help. Two examples are R. B. Rackham, *The Acts of the Apostles* (London: Methuen and Co., 1939), pp. 303-06; Leander E. Keck, *Mandate to Witness* (Valley Forge: The Judson Press, 1964), pp. 109-111, 114.

[2] Keck, *op. cit.*, p. 110. Used by permission.

[3] Thus the quotation from one of their poets, "For we are also his offspring," was interpreted in Christian terms, although originally phrased in pagan terms. It is frequently ascribed to Aratus, a Cilician Stoic, and is something of a creedal statement for stoicism. The idea of "offspring" centers in a natural relationship, and falls short of the "sonship" which the Christian enjoys with his heavenly Father.

[4] A similar reference in Acts 24:27 marks the change of governors in Caesarea.

A Mission Center:
Ephesus
Acts 18:18 to 21:14

A pastor may remain in one field for several years, minister faithfully, and extend his ministry quietly to mission points nearby. For his work he may receive scant recognition. Then he moves on. Perhaps this new work is larger; he receives more notice. Yet the pattern of his work is much the same as before. Who can say one work is more worthy than the other?

Paul's ministry in Ephesus receives more notice in Acts than did his work in other places. Luke used approximately 60 verses for Ephesus, as compared with 30 for Philippi; 18 for Corinth. Moreover, more of Paul's writings included in our New Testament were written from Ephesus than from any of the other centers we have studied. We cannot say, however, that Paul's ministry in Ephesus was his most important. Rather, we may say Paul's life in Ephesus was productive, perhaps even perilous.[1]

The Corinthian and Roman letters offer some detail on one of Paul's activities while he was in Ephesus: the collection for the poor in Jerusalem. This collection was a matter of great significance to Paul, but hardly noticed by Luke. Also, Christian tradition has attached importance to Ephesus as the site of one of Paul's imprisonments. If this is true, then some of the prison letters may have been sent from Ephesus, not Rome.[2]

From Ephesus Paul appears to have reached out into nearby communities. The Lycus River valley was inviting, especially the towns of Colossae, Hierapolis, and Laodicea. Perhaps some of Paul's friends went out from Ephesus to that area (Col. 2:1; 4:13). The capital of the province of Asia would be a natural center for such extension. Luke also included the work of Timothy and Erastus in Macedonia (19:22). Demetrius' charge (19:26) indicates that Paul's influence extended throughout the province.

1. Approach to Ephesus (18:18-23)

For many years Paul may have regarded Ephesus as a likely mission center. The visit to Cyprus with Barnabas and Mark had introduced an earlier mission to Galatia. After the Jerusalem Council Paul and Silas set out overland for a destination which may have been Ephesus. They reported the Council decisions to previously established churches, but then were "forbidden of the Holy Spirit to speak the word in Asia" (16:6). The Macedonian and Achaian ministries followed. In Corinth Paul appears to have settled for an intensive ministry, but Ephesus loomed ahead as a goal.

Paul took Aquila and Priscilla with him from Corinth. They were firm friends and valued co-workers. They purposely settled in Ephesus (18:19). While there on that first visit, Paul worshiped at the synagogue and offered his Christian witness. His ministry was limited by his plans, however; he promised to return at a later time. His Ephesian ministry was thus planned ahead; and his friends, Aquila and Priscilla, were left there to prepare the way. Paul set sail for Caesarea (vv. 21-22).

No details are recorded of Paul's visits to Caesarea, Jerusalem,[3] and Antioch, but his reports to each church must have been interesting. The fact that no information on these visits is available reminds us that Luke's treatment is not exhaustive. When Paul left Antioch, he moved overland toward the province of Asia. En route he visited Galatia and Phrygia, but this was only a prelude to the mission at Ephesus.

2. Ministry Among the Jews (18:24 to 19:9)

The Work of Aquila and Priscilla (18:24-28)
Aquila and Priscilla had remained in Ephesus, apparently to prepare for Paul's subsequent mission. An example of this preparation was their work with Apollos.

Apollos' visit to Ephesus reminds the reader that other workers, not related to the Pauline mission, were bearing the good news to the Mediterranean world. Apollos' education at Alexandria would have been of comparable quality with Paul's at Tarsus. Alexandria in Egypt had long been an educational center. The many Jews who had settled there took advantage of that fact.

Apollos lacked something in his Christian knowledge and experience, however. He accurately taught the facts of Jesus' life and ministry. He was enthusiastic and bold in his witness. Like Paul, he began his work in the synagogue. When they had heard Apollos, however, they knew he needed help. The kindly couple took him in and "expounded unto him the way of God more accurately" (v. 26).

When Apollos decided to go to Corinth, "the brethren encouraged him" (18:27). That phrase implies that more than Aquila and Priscilla were involved in this counsel. Likely, sympathetic Jews or Christians were related closely enough to Corinth to exert some influence there. In Corinth, Apollos surely came into close contact with Paul's interpretation of the gospel. There is evidence in the Corinthian letters (1 Cor. 1:12; 3:5,6,21-22; 4:6; 16:12), however, that Apollos' enthusiasm and, perhaps, immaturity created problems in that church.

This brief interlude (18:24-28) reveals some differences in early Christian thought. It also suggests the possibility that many Christian witnesses were at work. However, Luke—under the leadership of the Holy Spirit—helped make Paul's understanding and interpretation of the gospel the accepted teaching.

Paul and John the Baptist's Followers (19:1-7)

When Paul arrived at Ephesus, Apollos already had gone to Corinth (v. 1). In Ephesus Paul found disciples who did not fully understand the Christian faith (vv. 2-4). How these disciples were related to Apollos Luke does not record. The variety in Paul's ministry is underscored by his contact with them. A complete case history on the Ephesus disciples is impossible because important details are missing. We do know they lacked knowledge about the presence and work of the Holy Spirit. Perhaps they were zealous disciples of John the Baptist, as well as of Jesus. They knew of John's ministry, and of Jesus' ministry. However, they were baptized with a baptism signifying only their repentance. The Ephesus disciples had not received the Holy Spirit.

Did their belief represent a tradition from Alexandria? [4] Christian baptism symbolizes death to sin; it also symbolizes resurrection to new life. The Ephesus disciples' loyalty to a past and dead leader somehow had prevented a vital experience of the indwelling Lord. Paul placed in proper perspective John and Jesus, a perspective that John himself would have accepted (Luke 3:15-17). They were then baptized "into the name of the Lord Jesus" (v. 5). Paul "laid his hands upon them" (v. 6), and they gave evidence of the Holy Spirit's presence in their lives (v. 6).

In the Synagogue (19:8-9)

Consistent with earlier missions, Paul continued his work with the Jews. Aquila and Priscilla may have witnessed in the synagogue at Ephesus already; but when Paul arrived, the calm was broken. However, for a period of three months, Paul worked patiently in the synagogue. His subject with the Jews was the kingdom of God (v. 8), and he spoke clearly and courageously. As had been true elsewhere, opposition soon developed. For Paul to continue in the synagogue was impossible. He did not seek a showdown with Jewish leadership, however. He simply moved the Christian disciples to the school of Tyrannus. According to one manuscript, regular sessions at the school were limited to the morning and evening hours. Thus, the hall was available to Paul and his friends for the afternoon.

3. Success with the Gentiles (19:10-22)

Extent of Ministry (19:10)

In a single verse Luke summarized the Ephesian ministry: "All they that dwelt in Asia heard the word of the Lord, both Jews and Greeks" (v. 10). During this two-year period the mission's influence was extended from the capital city to the province as a whole. The hall of Tyrannus must have been a beehive of activity, although it is difficult to imagine Paul's being confined to one place. Asia was quite prominent in early church history; all the churches addressed in Revelation were in that province. To Paul's outreach must be added that of others, among them John, the exile of Patmos. He was well known in Ephesus. His activity, however, appears to be later than Paul's.

Representatives from Corinth came to visit Paul in Ephesus. It is possible that he, as well as his friends, made a visit to Corinth during this period. If these events occurred, Luke did not record them. Luke stressed Paul's settled Ephesian ministry, with his daily teaching in the hall of Tyrannus, and its wide influence. That ministry, after a while, began to antagonize both Jewish leaders and Gentile businessmen.

Paul's Mission Established (19:11-20)

After his summary statement (v. 10), Luke emphasized the supernatural power of the Christian faith. (Luke, for example, gave no details of Paul's ethical teachings, such as is contained in the letters to Corinth from Ephesus.) The Ephesians were attracted by these miraculous works. They interpreted them in terms of their own superstition. For instance, exorcism of demons was widely practiced in the ancient world. A group of Jewish exorcists witnessed Paul's casting out demons. Thereupon, seven sons of a Jewish priest named Sceva confronted a demoniac. They tried to cast out the demon by saying: "I adjure you by Jesus whom Paul preacheth" (v. 13).

One cannot read the account without appreciating the humor of the situation. The evil spirit replied: "Jesus I know, and Paul I know; but who are ye?" (v. 15). The evil spirit then attacked the seven men; they fled naked and bruised from the beating. The lessons from the episode are simple: (1) Spiritual power is not transferable, but must be derived from its source, the Holy Spirit; [5] (2) spiritual power is not in the words spoken, even in the use of Jesus' name, but in a vital relationship with him; and (3) spiritual power, even the evil kind, is greater than physical power. The story must have been repeated many times before Luke recorded it.

The miracles attracted many Jews and Greeks. Some were overawed by them; the name of Jesus was magnified. Some believed and openly confessed their sins and their faith. Some publicly put the torch to those books which had led them and others astray. The effect of the gospel in Asia was overwhelming. Its power over superstition established Paul's ministry in Ephesus. "So mightily grew the word of the Lord and prevailed" (v. 20).[6]

Future Plans (19:21-22)

Luke indicated that Paul had planned to leave Ephesus before the riot instigated by Demetrius occurred. (See vv. 21-22.) Paul's sense of direction seems to be clearer than at an earlier stage. He carried out well-laid plans. He looked forward to visiting Philippi, Thessalonica, Beroea, Athens, and Corinth. After that, Paul planned to journey to Jerusalem, where he would take the offering from the Gentile churches. Beyond that, Rome beckoned him westward. The imperial city must be visited.

Meanwhile Paul sent two trusted representatives, Timothy and Erastus, to Macedonia (v. 22). These probably were two of many that he dispatched from Ephesus to familiar and unfamiliar areas. Paul himself remained at the mission center.[7]

4. Trouble with Entrenched Interests (19:23-41)

The threads of religion and business in Ephesus were woven into a tight pattern. The worship of Artemis produced a demand for certain products. The manufacture of those products produced a profit. Thus, one reinforced the other. When these entrenched interests were threatened by the gospel, opposition came.

Partners in Worship and Business (19:23-27)

Demetrius was the leader of the silversmiths' guild in Ephesus. Their principal business was the manufacture of silver shrines in the form of the goddess, Artemis (Diana), or of her temple in Ephesus. The temple was one of the seven wonders of the ancient world, four times the size of the Parthenon. When it burned in the fourth century B.C., it was rebuilt immediately.[8] It served, not only as a shrine for worship, but as a bank for kings, cities, and individual citizens. The silver shrines were probably sold to worshipers, who presented them at the temple as an act of worship. Much of the silver could then be melted down and sold back to the silversmiths. Clearly, the temple cult, as well as the silversmiths, profited from the business. Any person who threatened their arrangement would be in danger.[9] This danger would be especially keen at the time of the Artemisia observance in March-April.

Riot at Ephesus (19:28-34)

About the time Timothy and Erastus departed for Macedonia, Paul appears to have moved to Asia with renewed vigor.[10] Demetrius' testimony (19:26) is a real compliment to the Christian mission. The converts from the worship of Diana to the Christian faith appear to have been many. Ephesus was ripe for a riot; the city was soon "filled with the confusion" (v. 29). The howling mob ("Great is Diana of the Ephesians") rushed against the Macedonians—Gaius and Aristarchus—who were members of Paul's company. The brief description of them as Paul's "companions in travel" (v. 29) indicates something of his outreach in the Ephesian ministry.

When Paul sought to enter the theater, designed to hold at least 24,000 people, friendly officials talked him out of it (v. 31). These officials—called Asiarchs—were leading men who promoted emperor worship in Asia. Delegates from the chief cities of each province made up a council which gave oversight to it. This worship was a political-religious cult, more political than religious. The president of the council acted as high priest and held office for one year. Apparently, Paul had become friendly with several of them. The confusion of the mob would have prevented Paul's making any logical presentation of his position. It was better that Paul did remain outside. To see that, one need only examine the crowd's response to Alexander, whom the Jews put forward in an effort to clear themselves. Anti-Semitism, combined with local loyalties, overwhelmed him with cries of praise to Diana.

Action of the Town Clerk (19:35-41)
Ephesus was a free city with a regularly scheduled town meeting. The authority at such a meeting rested in the town clerk. It was normal that he should address the crowd in the theater. His remarks, as recorded by Luke, were simple, and seemed to calm the assembly. They may be summarized as follows: Artemis (Diana) is goddess of Ephesus, regardless. Her image (perhaps a roughly hewn tree trunk decorated with carved breasts as a goddess of fertility) was known to have fallen "down from Jupiter" (v. 35). Neither Paul, Gaius, nor Aristarchus had defamed her. They had not robbed her temple. In addition, any charges should have been made in the courts, or before proconsuls. There were regular assembly dates for such matters. If Rome heard of this, woe be to Ephesus! (See vv. 35-41.)

After his remarks, the town clerk dismissed the assembly, and thus Paul's mission remained unchallenged by a responsible Roman official. Further preaching by Paul, however, only would have aggravated the tense situation. As it was, his opponents had been blamed with the riot. In any event, he had intended to leave. This was the right time.

The Christian faith has not always been so fortunate in its struggle with entrenched wealth and traditional worship.

5. Departure from Ephesus (20:1-16)

Through Macedonia and Greece (20:1-3)
Timothy and Erastus already had been sent to Macedonia. Now Paul followed them, going "through those parts" (20:2). Certainly the church in Philippi was thanked in person for its kindness. Beroea was given attention as well. A brief reference in 2 Corinthians 2:12 to a visit in Troas on the way to Macedonia may belong to this journey, although the Troas visit may have occurred earlier. The reference to Greece likely indicates Corinth rather than Athens. Paul spent three months there. It is generally supposed that the letter to the church at Rome was written during this period.[11]

Preparation for Offering (20:4-6)
The Jews' plot against Paul "as he was about to set sail for Syria" (v. 3) appears as a small cloud of the gathering storm in Jerusalem. Continually he had drawn Jews to Christ, and away from

their traditional worship. Moreover, he had created problems for Jews in both Corinth and Ephesus. There was, however, another area of great interest to the Jews. Ephesus was a center for the collection of Jewish gifts to the Temple at Jerusalem. Paul's ministry in Ephesus had been successful among Jews as well as Gentiles. His work may have hurt Temple offerings.

During the period of the Ephesian ministry (extending from Acts 18:18 to 20:38), Paul and his friends had been gathering funds for the poor in Jerusalem. He sensed that this ministry of essentially Gentile churches to the church at Jerusalem could bind the two segments of Christianity closer together. He sought to involve as many Gentile churches as possible.

Luke did not include an account of this offering in Acts.[12] Paul seemed to attach great significance to the offering in his letters (see Rom. 15:26; 1 Cor. 16:1-4; 2 Cor. 9:1-8). Although Luke did not deal with the offering, he did include the names of those who represented the various provinces in which Paul had labored (vv. 4-5). Likely, these persons bore gifts from the churches in those provinces, and accompanied Paul to Jerusalem.

Paul's care in the offering is notable (2 Cor. 8:19-22). It was taken in the churches of Galatia (1 Cor. 16:1), Achaia (1 Cor. 16:2; 2 Cor. 8:10-15), and Macedonia (2 Cor. 8:1-5). These references to the offering belong to the Ephesian ministry. Rome also was informed of Paul's plan (Rom. 15:25-27). The offering was a joint effort, many churches working together in Christ's mission.

A Visit to Troas (20:7-12)

Paul's original intent of sailing for Syria was altered by news of a plot by the Jews. The others sailed immediately for Troas and awaited Paul's arrival there after Passover. He hoped to be in Jerusalem about seven weeks later, in time for Pentecost (Acts 20:16). Significantly, the "us" is resumed in Acts 20:5, indicating that Luke had joined Paul for the voyage to Troas. Perhaps Paul told him about the riot at Ephesus at that time. This would explain the detail with which it is reported.

There is, in the account of the week-long stay at Troas, a priceless, though brief, account of a church service. Paul was likely waiting for a ship to Syria during the seven days mentioned (v. 6). On the first day of the week Christians gathered to break bread. Was this a regular meal, or is the reference to the Memorial Supper? The service probably came after the workday was completed. Paul preached the word until midnight (v. 7). Since Paul intended to depart the next day, an all-night vigil may have been planned. The place of the meeting was likely a private home, where a large upper room was available. Many oil lamps served for light, as well as ornamentation. (Jews began the sabbath day with the hanging of a lamp in the window, and Gentiles celebrated their festivals with many such lights.)

The heat and fumes of the many lamps were too much for a young man, Eutychus. Unfortunately, he sat in a window. Upon falling asleep, he tumbled to the earth below, and was judged to be dead by those who rushed to him. Acts reports Paul's ministry to Eutychus and his assurances to the other friends (v. 10). After a while the congregation resumed its service. They fellowshipped until daylight.

Bypassing Ephesus (20:13-16)
From this point the narrative reads almost like a traveler's diary. Luke stayed with the ship; Paul went part of the way by land, and part by ship. Perhaps the ship stopped each night. If so, that would explain Luke's careful reporting of the cities visited: Assos, Mitylene, Chios, Samos, and Miletus (vv. 14-15). Pentecost was approaching; therefore Paul could spend no time in Ephesus. Since Miletus was only thirty-six miles from Ephesus, Paul asked the Ephesian church leaders to meet him there (v. 17).

6. Charge to the Church Leaders (20:17-38)

Organization of church life in Ephesus appears to have been relatively simple. When Paul departed after the riot, he exhorted the "disciples" (20:1). From Miletus he sent for the "elders" (20:17). He had appointed elders in other churches as well (14:23). Paul appears to have followed the pattern of the Jewish synagogue in this matter. Luke does not seem to be overly concerned with the matter of church organization.

Paul's message is the only example we have in the New Testament of a sermon to church leaders. It is basically a pastoral charge. It may be divided into three parts: (1) Paul's review of his Ephesian ministry (vv. 18-27); (2) Paul's charge to the church leaders (vv. 28-31); and (3) Paul's farewell (vv. 32-35).

The Ephesian Ministry Reviewed (20:18-27)
All through this brief discourse (vv. 18-27), Paul may appear to the reader as somewhat defensive. After all, Paul's ministry at Ephesus had been stormy at points; always varied. However, he had been faithful in his public teaching, and in his house-to-house

ministry. He had presented the whole truth boldly. His life in their midst had been blameless. He had not been guilty of covetousness; he had supported his ministry with his tentmaking. Paul stressed these matters as he reviewed his relationship with the Ephesians. Perhaps he wanted to emphasize his motive, as well as his procedures. These church leaders could learn from his example.

Charge to Church Leaders (20:28-31)

Paul realized that his planned visit to Jerusalem was filled with danger, and that he might be speaking his final word to the Ephesian church leaders. His charge to the elders identified them as "bishops" (v. 28). The Revised Standard Version translates that word "guardians." The reference was to function, not office. The term means that the Holy Spirit had given them places of service; they were to minister faithfully to the members of the flock. It was the Lord's church, not that of the elders, nor even of Paul himself. The apostle consistently remembered his own place as a servant of the Lord in the church. So the elders were advised, "Take heed unto yourselves, and to all the flock" (v. 28). They were to "watch" (v. 31) their group lest perverse men arise from it; to "help the weak" (v. 35); and to "remember the words of the Lord Jesus" (v. 35). They were responsible for the welfare of the church.

Paul's Farewell (20:32-35)

Paul's words of farewell are not confined to the final verses. In fact, the entire discourse is a farewell address. The uncertainty Paul expressed about his visit to Jerusalem (vv. 22-23) is realistic. His appraisal suggests that Paul had kept up contacts with friends there. This visit, with its attempt to bind the Jewish and Gentile segments of the church together, would climax his mission (v. 24). Meanwhile, the church at Ephesus faced critical days. His love for it is made clear by his use of the pastoral figure: the flock would be threatened by wolves.[13]

Several unique features are included in Paul's brief words. He referred to a ministry of "three years" (v. 31) in Ephesus. This may be approximate, since only twenty-seven months are actually accounted for. The reference to God's grace as "able to build you up, and to give you the inheritance among all them that are sanctified" (v. 32) appears to reflect Paul's own experience. A word of Jesus, which does not appear elsewhere in the New Testament, is included: "It is more blessed to give than to receive" (v. 35). This beatitude did not find its way into the beatitudes of either Matthew or Luke. It is certainly a clear reflection of Jesus' ministry, and was a guideline for Paul's own ministry at Ephesus and elsewhere.

The church leaders sensed the finality of the farewell, and tearfully saw Paul aboard the ship for Syria. This marks the end of the Ephesian ministry, the longest, and likely the most productive, in the apostle's career.

7. Going to Jerusalem (21:1-14)

Luke's interest in the details of travel becomes more apparent as his account continues. It is easy to plot the course of the party on a map of the first-century Mediterranean area. Paul did not travel on chartered vessels; his was a cargo ship. He found friends everywhere, and this slowed his journey. In Tyre, although there is no account of a former ministry there, he quickly "found the disciples" (21:4) and remained for a week. Few details of this meeting are preserved, but we do know that his friends warned of the dangers in Jerusalem (v. 4). Paul's course was set, however. His friends in Tyre saw him board the ship for Ptolemais, and then they returned home (vv. 5-6). Paul remained in Ptolemais for a day.

Caesarea was the site of a longer stay for Paul (23:33 to 26:32). A central figure among the Christians at Caesarea was Philip, one of the seven men selected in Jerusalem for the ministry to the widows (6:5). After his effective preaching in Samaria, and his personal witness to the Ethiopian eunuch, he made Caesarea his home.

While Paul was visiting with Philip, the prophet Agabus (11:28; 21:10) came down from Jerusalem, and in a symbolic act warned of the danger in Jerusalem. The symbolism was typical of Jewish prophets. It was a sharp reminder of the peril ahead. At this point Luke joined the group in trying to dissuade Paul. (See Luke's use of "us" in v. 11.) Other church leaders might have taken the gifts from Gentile churches to Jerusalem, but Paul insisted that he be a part of this task. At Paul's insistence his friends ceased pleading. They declared simply, "The will of the Lord be done" (21:14).

The number of verses Luke devoted to the Ephesian ministry indicates its significance. It also allows a detailed account of the great events that took place there. The first incident was Paul's instruction of the twelve disciples; the last, the tearful scene at Miletus. The action in between those events reflects the widening influences of the gospel, and the grave peril which developed for Christian leaders when the gospel threatened the status quo.

The events in Ephesus depict Paul as working from a settled base. Although he moved about Asia, possibly going so far as Corinth in Achaia, Ephesus was the center. Paul's personal influence, through the work done by his representatives and himself, extended throughout the province of Asia. Paul's work in Ephesus portrays him as maturing in his ministry.

Luke omitted events, to be sure, but that truth underscores two facts: (1) Those events did not fit into Luke's purpose; and (2) Paul's letters supplement Acts with helpful details. Demetrius' accusation, "Almost throughout all Asia, this Paul hath persuaded and turned away much people" (19:26), simply confirms Luke's earlier statement, "All they that dwelt in Asia heard the word of the Lord" (19:10).

8. Truth for Today

Immaturity in Christian thought and growth offers an opportunity to pastor and people. Aquila, Priscilla, and Paul dealt patiently with Apollos and the twelve Ephesian disciples. A nominal Christian is as much in need of the whole gospel as one who has never heard it!

In Christian work, the goal to win people to Christ is constant; the tactics may change. For Paul to have moved out of the synagogue was better than to have continued to antagonize the Jews by staying to preach there. Churches, church leaders, and Christian workers sometimes need to face changing situations with Paul's kind of courage and flexibility.

The power of the gospel affects all of a person's life. The books which a person reads may bind his mind. When certain of the Ephesians became Christian, they burned their books which contained pagan ideas. Christians should read wholesome material. However, the Christian need fear no truth, only half-truths. They are dangerous if not recognized for what they are.

A pastor or a church can expect opposition when vested interests are challenged. Social, economic, and cultural institutions may exact a terrible price from the individual or the church which challenges their authority or threatens their influence. The challenge, however, must be accepted.

Great care and orderliness ought to characterize the receiving and using of church funds. The church is a steward of the gifts with which it has been entrusted. It should merit the confidence of those who support it. Absolute honesty must prevail; the shadow of suspicion must be avoided.

A wise pastor deals personally and patiently with church leadership. He realizes that the church will survive his departure, and that his good influence can best be conserved through the lay leaders. If he remains, he increasingly will depend on these leaders. Therefore, leader training is an important need which must be met.

Many persons and groups are involved in Christ's mission. Each makes his contribution, then steps down. The mission of Christ, however, goes on!

---

[1] First Corinthians 15:32; 2 Corinthians 1:8-10; 4:8-9 reveal more difficulties than Luke included in Acts.

[2] George S. Duncan, *St. Paul's Ephesian Ministry* (New York: Charles Scribner's Sons, 1930). Dr. Duncan has collected and interpreted these traditions. He has written persuasively, relating them to the material included in the Acts and in Paul's New Testament letters.

[3] A visit to Jerusalem was always "up." This reference certainly means a visit to that church: "He went up and saluted the church" (v. 22).

[4] Frank Stagg, *The Book of Acts* (Nashville: Broadman Press, 1955), pp. 197-98. In this material Dr. Stagg discusses the possibility that Apollos' teaching came from training he had received in Alexandria, of North Africa.

[5] This problem had been confronted previously by Simon Peter in the request of Simon the magician (Acts 8:18-24).

[6] Paul S. Minear, "Dear Theo," *Interpretation,* 27 (1973), 131-150. In this article Dr. Minear asks the simple question, "Over what did it prevail?" (p. 135). He contends that the "word of the Lord" prevailed over disease and superstition.

[7] The movements of Paul during this period may include a visit to Corinth. (Second Cor. 2:12-14; 12:14; 13:1 look forward to a third visit.) Titus, not mentioned in the Acts account, was one of Paul's representatives to Corinth, as was "the brother whose praise in the gospel is spread through all the churches" (2 Cor. 8:18).

[8] From *The New Westminster Dictionary of the Bible,* edited by Henry Snyder Gehman. Copyright © MCMLXX, The Westminster Press. Used by permission. The name Diana is familiar to most students of mythology as the Roman goddess of the moon or of the chase. It is unfortunate that Artemis of Ephesus should have been confused with Diana. Artemis "was the mother-goddess of Asia Minor. . . . Her image was supposed to have fallen from heaven (Acts 19:35), and it may have been originally a meteoric stone. Its form is known from ancient coins as the rude figure of a woman with crowned head, many breasts, and extended arms supported by props."

[9] Leander E. Keck, *Mandate to Witness* (Valley Forge: The Judson Press, 1964), p. 143. Used by permission. Dr. Keck points out the threat to Ephesus in Paul's work: "The goddess was in danger, and therefore the city was threatened (19:23-27). Declining business was only a symptom of the disease. Here we see clearly how religion, business, and patriotism are interwoven. To threaten the worship of the goddess would not only affect the economy but would endanger the security of the community."

[10] First Corinthians 16:8-9 possibly refers to this period: "I will tarry

at Ephesus until Pentecost, for a great door and effectual is opened unto me, and there are many adversaries."

[11] Romans 15:23 characterizes Paul's ministry in that area as completed; Romans 15:24 indicates an interest in the world beyond Rome.

[12] There is a reference to an offering in Paul's defense before Felix (Acts 24:17, and perhaps in Acts 20:35). However, Luke does not discuss the offering in Acts, nor Paul's activity in its behalf.

[13] Minear, *op. cit.,* pp. 148-49. Professor Minear identifies the "wolves" as those "whose patterns of Christian leadership diverge from Paul's: his humility and tears, his readiness to accept trials, his willingness to be martyred, his innocence of their blood . . .. In this long valedictory there is only one phrase that suggests doctrinal subversion (v. 30) and there are a dozen clauses that implicitly accuse the wolves of such crimes as greed, pride, and blindness to community needs . . .. Luke writes as a theologian, of course, but also as a pastoral theologian concerned with the pastoral obligations of 'ministers of the word.' "

Christ's Unfettered Witness:
Jerusalem to Rome

Acts 21:15 to 28:31

Stone walls do not a prison make, nor iron bars a cage." [1]
The poet described a freedom of the spirit which rises above
physical bonds. The words might have been written of Paul, and
of others who, in the early years of the church, were imprisoned
for the sake of the gospel. The more completely Christ possessed
a witness, the less galling his bonds became. Who is wearing the
fetters in these final chapters of Acts is not always clear. Is it
the judged, or the judging? Although the story moves relentlessly
toward Paul's arrest and imprisonment, no sense of the tragic
weighs on the reader. Instead, the material glows with triumph
and fulfillment. This is the story of how the Spirit of God worked
to free the gospel from its early constraints, imposed by the Jewish
Christians in Jerusalem.

1. Jerusalem: Love (21:15 to 23:30)

The action of this last section of Acts begins in Jerusalem. Paul's
strategy in gathering funds from Gentile churches for Jerusalem's
needs required his presence in Jerusalem. Paul's vision for the
church included free and open relations between Jewish and Gentile believers. The offering was to help make that vision reality.
That his purpose failed is disappointing. Later developments,
however, proved Paul's failure included a blessing: The gospel
was freed of Jewish legalism. God overruled Paul in favor of an
unfettered gospel.

Report to James and the Church (21:17-26)
The exciting reports of Paul's mission in the province of Asia contrast sharply with the dullness of church life in Jerusalem. The

125

w of the modern Appian Way, the traditional
vhere Roman Christians met Paul.

situation there does not appear to have changed. James and the
elders were still in control. Paul told of the Gentiles' conversion.
They heard him out, and rejoiced a bit (vv. 18-19). Then they
turned to more pressing matters: the pacification of the Jews
(vv. 20-24).

Conditions in Jerusalem were ripe for revolt against Rome.
From the standpoint of the Jerusalem church, the counsel the Jewish church leaders gave Paul was wise (vv. 20-24). As early as
the procuratorship of Ventidius Cumanus (A.D. 48-52) bad ad-
ministration had caused unrest. Felix succeeded him in 52 by
appointment from Emperor Claudius. Although Felix openly had
supported the Jews earlier, he was unfit as a ruler. A part of his
problem was his marriage to Drusilla, sister of Herod Agrippa II.

Josephus [2] wrote of many uprisings by the Jews against the
Romans. One of the most popular was led by an Egyptian Jew.
At the Mount of Olives he told his followers that he would make
the walls of Jerusalem fall down, and then he would inaugurate
the messianic kingdom. All the moderate Jews shrank from such
excesses. They feared Roman reprisal. Even Christian Jews were
caught in an either-or situation. They were identified in part with
the Gentile mission and with antilegalism. Hence, James was concerned that the church in Jerusalem appear to be zealous for the
law. Such action would tend to clear the Christians from Roman
suspicion.

Potential opposition to Paul among the Jews was clear. The
Sadducees, traditional enemies of the church, hated this Temple
robber. They despised his offerings for the poor almost as much
as his insistence on the resurrection of Jesus. The Pharisees were
more inclined to be sympathetic, but the moderate element was
rapidly losing control of the situation. The Sicarii, or Assassins,
were murderously anti-Rome, anti-Gentile, but pro-Jewish. At
festive occasions Jews returned to Jerusalem in large numbers. At
this Pentecost many would come from Asia and would report
Paul's successes in their region. The plot against him at Corinth
(20:3) reflects opposition from the Jews of the dispersion.

Within the church Jewish Christians would obey James. Yet
they were serving in the Jewish mission of Christianity. From the
outset it was probable that they would keep hands off. There
would be no active opposition to Paul from within the church,
only separation from him. James himself reminded Paul that he
was now in Jerusalem. His advice to Paul was simple: Line yourself up with the Jews; we'll manage the Gentiles. Had they not

written their judgment from the Jerusalem Council (15:28-29; 21:25)?

James' suggestion that Paul assume financial responsibility for four Jews under a vow may well reflect the difficulties of the relationship. Was the suggestion made to control Paul? to save him from possible trouble? to satisfy the Jews? to protect Jewish Christians? Expenses were not inconsequential in such religious ceremonies. Perhaps James decided that Paul's sharing of Gentile offerings with the church at Jerusalem indicated real wealth.[3] The vow was probably a temporary Nazirite dedication [4] in which the Jews lived as Nazirites for a short time. At the end of the period they shaved their beards, burned their hair, and offered the proper sacrifices: "the lambs, a ram, bread, cakes, and meat and drink offerings for each person." [5] (See Num. 6:13-20.) If, during the vow, those who had taken it became defiled in any manner, they had to spend seven more days in purification. At the end of that period, they were required to shave their heads and bring additional offerings to the priest. This burden was frequently assumed by the wealthy for special merit. Paul assumed the purification expenses for himself and four others. It was, in effect, one last effort to placate the Jewish wing of the church, and the unbelieving Jews.

Arrest (21:27-39)

Gentiles were forbidden to enter the Court of Israel in the Temple. Indeed, a Gentile entered any part of the Temple area at great peril. Paul appeared in the streets of Jerusalem with Asian Gentiles, known to Asian Jews. Later, he appeared in the Temple with persons unknown to the Asian Jews. Paul's enemies assumed these Jews to be Gentiles, whose presence in the Temple was contrary to Jewish law. The ensuing riot bears a striking similarity to the demonstration at Ephesus. (The name had changed: "Great is the Temple of the Jews!") The link between religious and economic interests was not unlike that in Ephesus.

The riddle of the closed Temple doors (21:30) is intriguing. The crowd had become violent; perhaps they were shut to prevent Paul's seeking sanctuary. Perhaps they were shut to protect the sanctity of the Temple. Roman soldiers were always conspicuous at festive seasons; always suspicious of a Jewish outbreak. They rushed to break up the crowd, and rescued Paul whom they saw at its center. He appears to have been blamed immediately. The bonds (v. 33) indicate that the military tribune assumed Paul's guilt.

Paul addressed the chief military officer in Greek, a fact that surprised him. The officer had assumed that Paul was the noted Egyptian troublemaker of the time (v. 38). Paul identified himself as a Jew, and as a citizen of Tarsus (v. 39). (He did not make his Roman citizenship clear to the officer until the interview described in 22:25-29. When the officer learned that fact, he proved to be one of Paul's allies. The officer, however, only intended to enforce the Roman law; any benefits to Paul were incidental.)

Appeal on the Castle Stairs (21:40 to 22:29)

Paul's defense took place on the stairs leading from the Temple portico upward to the Tower of Antonia, a Roman fortress overlooking the Temple courts. It had long been occupied by Roman soldiers, and at festive seasons the number was increased. The defense (22:3-21) itself is something of a personal witness: This happened to me. Paul, although in bonds, spoke freely:

"I am a Jew" (v. 3). He was a Jew of the dispersion, trained by the highly respected Gamaliel (v. 3). "I persecuted this Way unto the death" (v. 4). His persecution of the Christians did not reflect the gentle, tolerant spirit of his teacher, Gamaliel, however. Paul's zealous efforts in behalf of the law easily could be verified in Temple records.

"There shone from heaven a great light round about me" (v. 6). Paul's simple account of conversion is quite effective. There is no effort to explain it, nor to go into details. The Lord spoke, and Paul obeyed.

"One Ananias . . . came unto me" (vv. 12-13). Ananias was a law-abiding Jew. One of the unique features in this account of Paul's conversion is the long charge by Ananias.

"I will send thee forth far hence unto the Gentiles" (v. 21). Paul's report of his vision in the Temple is a unique presentation of his call to the Gentiles (see 9:26-30). His presence in the Temple area at the time of this defense made it particularly apt. The suggestion that the Temple could be the origin of the mission to the Gentiles angered the Jews. This was the point— the mission to the Gentiles—with which they took issue.

Paul's defense was a witness, simply and clearly stated: This happened to me. How could one improve on such a personal confession or a clear Christian witness? The Jews understood that the Gentile mission had its origin in Paul's Temple experience. There was no shaking his conviction on the rightness of that mission. Therefore they rejected Paul, and his entire concept (vv.

22-23). The military officer removed Paul from their presence (v. 24).

While being prepared for examination by scourging, Paul made clear his Roman citizenship. To the Roman officer's surprise, Paul was a "Roman born" (v. 28), his father having been a citizen before him. Roman citizenship was a highly desirable prize. Many purchased it, as had the officer. Although not released, Paul was treated with respect by his new ally. Already Paul was beginning to be freed from the bonds of Jewish prejudice.

Hearing Before the Sanhedrin (22:30 to 23:10)

The secular powers could find no guilt in Paul, any more than Pilate had found guilt in Jesus (see Luke 23:13-16). Therefore, the commanding officer ordered the Sanhedrin convened so that he might know the cause of the conflict. Before the Sanhedrin Paul declared his innocence (23:1). Presiding was Ananias, high priest by the grace of Rome (A.D. 47-59). Paul's appeal to his good conscience almost comprises a separate witness to his innocence. The high priest reacted quickly in the face of that which he regarded as blasphemy (v. 2).

Several questions are provoked by Paul's sharp attack on Ananias (vv. 3-5). Did Paul not know that he was high priest? Was his seat not obvious in the council chamber, or was Paul's eyesight poor, or was this sarcasm? Was Paul's lack of knowledge due to the short time he had spent in Jerusalem? We have no sure answers to these questions.

Sensing the impossibility of justice in the situation, Paul appealed to the division in the council: He set Pharisee against Sadducee on the subject of the resurrection (v. 6). It was a desperate act, and emphasized the break between Paul and the Jews. His long experience convinced him that he could be destroyed by their prejudice. He chose to use their prejudice to set them against each other (vv. 7-9). Once again the Roman officer rescued Paul from religious people (v. 10).

Plot Against Paul (23:11-30)

Paul himself must have had second thoughts about the scene before the Sanhedrin. He had been unable to witness effectively there, and actually had turned them in upon themselves. It was time for divine reassurance. God spoke the needed words (23:11); Paul was assured that he would live to witness in Rome.

A plot against Paul was nothing new (20:3). The significant feature in Acts 23:12-16 is that Paul's nephew overheard the plotters. Was the young man known to, and acceptable to, this band of fanatics? Did Paul's family have connections with the Jewish conspirators? These Sicarii (Assassins) were responsible for the death of many Jews and Romans during the period prior to the Jewish-Roman War. Little is known about Paul's family, but it certainly had some interesting connections!

Paul's confidence in the Roman officer is indicated in his sending his nephew to report the plot (v. 17). The officer believed the nephew's account and acted responsibly upon it (vv. 22-31). With great care the tribune prepared for the journey to Caesarea. The situation in Jerusalem was explosive, and a Roman citizen's life was in jeopardy. It was hardly a pious act on the tribune's part. It was good politics, as his letter to Governor Felix reveals. The officer may have hoped for a promotion.

The tribune's letter began: "Claudius Lysias unto the most excellent governor Felix, greeting" (v. 26). It was a typical first-century letter, brief and to the point. Similar official letters have been discovered among first-century papyri. Of course, Lysias portrayed himself in the best possible light. God appears to have been using Roman politics to accomplish his own purpose.

For love of his people Paul had interrupted his westward journey and returned to Jerusalem. His behavior appears to have been exemplary. He accepted James' suggestion that he align himself with law-abiding Jews. From that point on, however, James and the church at Jerusalem seem to have washed their hands of Paul. Paul's love for his people, although rejected in Jerusalem, is clear even in Rome, as we shall see (Acts 28:17-24). At great personal risk and sacrifice Paul sought to win both Gentile and Jew.

2. Caesarea: Boldness (23:31 to 26:32)

Herod the Great had built Caesarea on the site of an older town, and had constructed such extensive harbor facilities that the port was known far and wide. The governor lived there. Because of the feeling against Paul in Judea, his transfer to Caesarea was logical. Luke's presentation of the Roman officials' series of inquiries, and Paul's defenses, strengthen the legal standing of the Christian faith in Roman law. It is probably designed to be an appeal to the truth of history in a time of unjust persecution by the imperial government. The account shows that the church had always been loyal to the empire; that this loyalty had been confirmed by many Romans in official positions.

Defense Before Felix (24:1-23)
The zeal with which the Jewish religious powers proceeded against Paul is remarkable. Apparently Tertullus was a prosecutor of renown. His reported accusations portray both skill and insight (24:2-8). The indictment is threefold: (1) Paul had disturbed the peace all over the world; (2) he was a ringleader among the Nazarenes, a Jewish dissident sect; and (3) he had brought Gentiles into the forbidden Temple area. Thus the charges were political, religious, and specific.[6]

Paul's defense followed the same lines as the accusation. He is portrayed as more forthright, and less self-conscious than Tertullus. The emphasis on the ability of the Christian spokesman to control himself under duress is clear. That he was a Christian he admitted immediately, but denied any violation of Roman law. His devotion to Jewish institutions was undeniable, even to the extent of his participating in the Temple vows. Paul's mention of "alms" and "offerings" (v. 17) may refer to the gifts of the Gentile churches. If so, it is Luke's only reference to that offering.

Paul concluded his defense with a reference to his having divided the Sanhedrin on the question of the resurrection (v. 21). This action with the Sanhedrin was hardly cause for indictment in a Roman hearing, a fact that all present knew. Certainly Felix knew more about "the Way" (v. 22) than the Jews suspected. He postponed a decision until more information was available on Paul's behavior in Jerusalem. This information awaited the coming of Claudius Lysias, the Roman officer responsible for putting Paul in the state's custody.

Interview with Felix and Drusilla (24:24-27)
Members of the Herodian family were noted for their political acumen and their personal immortality. Such an Herodian was Drusilla, wife of Felix. She had been married to Azizus of Emesa, but sensed a better alliance with Felix. She deserted her husband for the Roman governor. It is probable that the Jewess was curious about Paul. As he spoke of "righteousness, and self-control, and the judgment to come" (v. 25), Felix was self-condemned. It is possible that the Herodian princess had been hardened to such prophetic judgments. As John the Baptist had condemned the adultery of an earlier Herod, so Paul spoke a word of judgment.

Felix may have been fascinated by Paul's forthrightness. Luke charges Felix's interest in Paul to the hope for a bribe from him (v. 26). It is strange that Luke should so accuse a Roman governor except that Felix had fallen into disrepute by Luke's time. Be-

cause of his handling of a Jewish-Syrian riot in Caesarea, in which
some Jews had been killed, Felix was recalled to Rome. Had it
not been for his desire to placate the Jews after this experience,
Felix might have released Paul.

Defense Before Festus (25:1-12)

After two years Felix was replaced by Festus. There is no evidence
of the Jerusalem church members' remembering Paul after that
lapse of time. Not so the Jewish leaders, who immediately accused
Paul before the new governor. Having resented Paul's removal
from their jurisdiction, they plotted to kill him. Luke carefully
portrayed the new Roman governor as fair and impartial. To
the Jewish leader's plan Festus replied that Paul was in Caesarea; his accusation could be presented there (vv. 4-6). Later in
Caesarea the Jews appear to have exaggerated their accusations
(v. 7). Festus, not being so familiar with Jewish customs as his
predecessor, suggested to Paul that he go to Jerusalem for a
hearing (v. 9).

With reluctance Paul appealed to Caesar (vv. 11-12). This
appeal came only after a two-year confinement in Caesarea, and
the frustrating experience of the hearing before the new governor.
His appeal put Paul in a bad light with the Jews: He had renounced the Jewish ideal of theocracy. His statement in Rome
underscores the reluctance with which Paul made that appeal
(28:19). He knew that there was no chance of a just hearing
before the Jewish religious leaders. Rather, he simply would be
made a present to the Assassins. Thus Paul, a Roman citizen,
placed himself at the mercy (and justice) of the Roman emperor.
Festus concurred in Paul's request; Paul's course was set (v. 12).

Defense Before Agrippa and Bernice (25:13 to 26:32)

Agrippa II and Bernice's visit of state set the stage for Paul's
next bold defense in Caesarea. Agrippa II was a son of Agrippa I,
and ruled over Chalcis and certain other areas in northern Palestine.
These territories originally belonged to Philip, who was a son of
Herod the Great, and uncle to Agrippa I. Agrippa I succeeded
Philip. When Agrippa I died, Agrippa II was not old enough to receive his father's kingdom. He came to power four years later,
in A.D. 48.

Bernice was Agrippa II's sister. She had been married to their
uncle, but at the time of her husband's death she was reputed
by the Jews to have formed an incestuous relationship with her
brother, Agrippa II. That rumored relationship fired the Jews'
dislike of Agrippa. A further basis for his disfavor with the

Jews was his appointment of a new Jewish high priest. He had deposed Ananias. This action was regarded by the Jews as a misuse of power.

Festus' description of Paul's case to Agrippa makes clear the injuries Paul had suffered (vv. 14-21). The governor is portrayed by Luke as careful at two points: Paul's apparent innocence of any crime; Festus' handling of the case in a wise and fair manner. In his discussion of the case, Festus stressed the unusual aspects. Agrippa expressed interest; a hearing for Paul before the king was set (v. 22).

The pomp and ceremony of the hearing appear to have been a mockery of the justice which Roman law acquired. Paul made an able defense before Agrippa and Bernice. Actually, he presented a summary statement of his life in Judaism and his conversion experience. Although Paul must have been discouraged by this time, he used the opportunity to witness to a reigning Jew, and a member of the famous Herodian family. His deference to the king's position (perhaps in the light of his knowledge that the high priest, Ananias, had been deposed) suggests that Paul may have sensed hope in the situation, even though he had already appealed to Caesar. On the other hand, the fact of his appeal to Caesar may have left him free to present his gospel to Agrippa.

As a Jew, Paul had been guiltless. His compliance with the Jewish law was above reproach. The account of his zeal as a Pharisee underscored the miracle of his conversion. A classic description of the conversion experience appears in verse 18. Paul's movement from darkness to light, from Satan to God, and his receiving of forgiveness and an inheritance with other believers—this was Paul's understanding of conversion. He needed to make no apology about his mission to the Gentiles to one so urbane as Agrippa. His obedience to the vision, and his faithful witness, provoked the opposition of the Jews in Jerusalem. Agrippa knew them to be an unruly crowd.

Festus interrupted Paul when he mentioned the resurrection. Paul's witness to the resurrection appears to have provoked a very definite response (v. 24).

Paul had clearly directed his defense to Agrippa for the purpose of gaining a convert. The old missionary was chomping at the bit. Here was a potential convert, and a Jewish ruler at that! Agrippa appears to have sensed Paul's purpose. His response to Paul has been understood variously. The translation "Almost thou persuadest" (v. 28, KJV) has provided the text for a well-known gospel song. Other versions translate differently: "With but little persuasion" (ASV); "In a short time" (RSV); "In this short time" (TEV). The phrase refers to Agrippa's recognition of Paul's purpose: "You think it will not take much to win me over and make a Christian of me" (v. 28, NEB).

Both Festus and Agrippa, Roman governor and Jewish king, agreed: Paul was innocent of any wrongdoing. However, he had appealed to Caesar, and to Caesar he would go. Is there a hint of Luke's disappointment with Paul's appeal to Caesar?

3. Aboard Ship: Faith (27:1 to 28:14)

Paul's voyage, including the shipwreck, is a travelogue of lasting interest.[7] Luke has preserved nautical details which modern sailors find both accurate and intriguing. It is possible that Luke was an amateur sailor himself. His primary purpose, however, was to present Paul as a Christian in crisis. He was in command of the situation, and he made friends of the company with which he traveled. His faith was strong even under duress.

Caesarea to Myra: A Christian and His Friends (27:1-5)
Paul was not the only prisoner going to Rome, but Paul was singled out from the beginning as responsible. The centurion, Julius, treated him kindly. Paul was permitted the company of at least two old friends, the author (Luke) and Aristarchus. Perhaps these went along to minister to his needs, as well as to be his companions in travel. At Sidon, some sixty-seven miles from Caesarea, and the first port of call, Julius allowed Paul to disembark and visit with friends (v. 3). The variety of ships in the voyage suggests the vast amount of travel in the ancient world, as well as the volume of materials transported from Mediterranean ports to Rome. Putting to sea again, the ship encountered contrary winds (v. 4).

Myra to Fair Havens: A Christian Subject to Nature (27:6-8)
The ship from Alexandria was loaded with wheat. Grain ships were necessarily large. Perhaps it had been forced to Myra by the contrary winds, but now moved more directly toward Rome. With great difficulty in the face of the wind, prevailingly northwest, they sailed under the lee of Crete. The account suggests that the author looked back over the experience as exciting. Perhaps he and Paul reminisced many times about the rough crossing.

Fair Havens to Cauda: A Christian and Skilled Seamen (27:9-17)
Skilled sailors could direct a ship's progress almost into the teeth of

the wind, but it took time. Since the season for sailing was already far advanced, Paul cautioned the centurion and the crew to winter in Fair Havens (v. 10). Perhaps Fair Havens did not offer as much entertainment as Phoenix, or perhaps the harbor was safer at Phoenix. Whatever the case, the crew would not listen to advice from a prisoner, even though he had both experience and insight. The south shore of Crete is protected by the White Mountains (elevation 9,000 feet). A south wind would have seemed a real advantage as they sailed along, close to the shore of the island.

The sudden change of the wind subjected the ship to violent force; they were driven off course to the island of Cauda. The small lifeboat they had been towing was secured while they were protected from the tempestuous wind by the island (v. 16). The hull of the ship was strengthened by undergirding (v. 17). Fearful of the quicksands off the northern coast of Africa, they allowed themselves to be driven by the wind in a westerly direction, and away from Cauda (v. 17).

Cauda to Melita: A Christian and His Courage (27:18-44)
As the voyage progressed, Paul expressed his opinion more forcefully. At the time of the shipwreck Paul appears to have been in command (vv. 31-35). While others, including experienced seamen, were terrified at the force of the storm, Paul courageously insisted there would be no loss of life.

For many days they did not eat. Paul spoke encouragingly on the basis of his faith. We cannot know how much confidence he inspired among the sailors. Finally, having been driven back and forth in the area where the Mediterranean and the Adriatic Seas come together, the sailors reckoned that land was near. In an effort to prevent being driven on the rocks, anchors were put out from the stern of the ship. Thus the seamen were assured some respite from the winds.

Morning came, and the sailors planned to desert ship. Paul cautioned Julius that the sailors must remain with the ship. Thereupon, the soldiers cut the ropes holding the dinghy and thus prevented the sailors' escape. Paul's courage in counseling the crew and passengers to eat was based on his faith that there would be no loss of life. The 276 aboard ate all they could, then lightened the ship further by throwing the rest of the provisions overboard. Just when it seemed that the ship might be saved, it ran aground and began to break up in the sea (vv. 39-41).

When shipwreck was inevitable, the soldiers planned to kill the prisoners. It was better that the prisoners be killed (the soldiers thought) than for the soldiers to be blamed for the prisoners' escape. Julius, having developed a healthy respect, if not friendship, for Paul, intervened. All escaped to land—the island of Malta (Melita).

Melita to Puteoli: A Christian and His Compassion (28:1-14)
Since the wind and the rain made a fire necessary, Paul joined the others in gathering wood (vv. 1-5). While Paul was tending the fire, a viper fastened itself to his hand. The others of the company became alarmed. Paul was not harmed, however, and the natives were impressed. Perhaps Paul's sailing companions had come to expect this sort of good fortune where he was concerned.

Luke took delight in describing the healing of the chief's father. Paul seemed to have had a hand in the company's safety from shipwreck. He had survived the viper. Now the apostle attended a sick man. Perhaps Dr. Luke had diagnosed the case as fever and dysentery. Whatever the case, Paul's prayer and laying on of hands became God's means for healing the old man. Paul and his companions were held in honor by all.

From Melita (Malta) they sailed to Syracuse, where they waited for a favorable wind. From there they arrived finally at Puteoli, seaport of Naples. There, as a good omen for the future, they found brethren (v. 14). Surely the word describes believers like themselves. For seven days they visited with them.

4. Rome: Freedom (28:15-31)

"And so we came to Rome" (v. 14). Luke presents the coming to Rome as something of a triumphal entry. The freedom which Paul enjoyed marked him as an exceptional prisoner (vv. 16,31).

Received by Brethren (28:15-16)
More brethren journeyed to the suburbs of Rome to meet them, for word of Paul's arrival had reached the Christians of the city. After the long, tiring voyage new friends were especially welcome. The gospel had arrived in Rome well before Paul. The church was already there; he had written to it some years earlier. Luke was more concerned with Paul's arrival in Rome than with the details of how the good news itself arrived. Perhaps he did not know that story. Did some unknown traveler first proclaim Christ in the imperial city? Many were working in Christ's mission.

Meeting with Jewish Leaders (28:17-22)
In spite of all Paul's difficulties with Jewish leaders, he invited them to his dwelling. Was Luke impatient with the apostle's con-

cern for his Jewish brethren? The gospel was for the world, the
center of which was Rome. Yet in Rome, Paul met first with
Jewish leaders! The meeting with the Jews in Rome indicates
that Paul planned a ministry there, in spite of his bonds.

Apparently, Paul's appeal to Caesar in rejection of his own
people and their judicial system continued to concern him. He pro-
tested his innocence on all counts, and emphasized the Roman
officials' willingness to release him, except for the Jews' accusation. The defense was unnecessary. The Jews in Rome had
received no information about Paul. It is difficult to believe that
neither letter nor visitor from Jerusalem had mentioned Paul's
case to these Jewish leaders. Rome was a large city, however, and
the Jews may have kept to a ghetto-type existence. They knew
little about the Christian faith. They set a time to learn more
about it.

Second Meeting with Jews (28:23-28)
When the appointed day arrived, a more formal meeting occurred.
Again they came to Paul's lodging. He used texts from the Old
Testament, much like Jesus himself after his resurrection (Luke
24:27). All day long Paul taught, and some believed.

Since some did not believe, Paul turned to the prophet Isaiah
for an explanation of this rejection. This passage is quoted often
in the New Testament. The quotation (Isa. 6:9-10) is a part of
Isaiah's call to the prophetic ministry. The prophet's task was not
to be easy; nor was Paul's. From city to city he had witnessed the
Jews' rejection of their Messiah. Now in Rome he turned again
to the Gentiles.[8]

Freedom for Preaching in Rome (28:30-31)
At first glance the concluding verses appear to leave the reader
hanging. Is there indeed an incompleteness about the Acts? Or is
the final scene so designed as to warm the audience with the assurance that the gospel has triumphed? Paul had wanted to preach in
Rome. For two years he enjoyed freedom to do just that. Beyond
those years, Luke is silent.[9]

The freedom which Paul experienced was possible because he
did not pose a threat to vested interests. In the provinces the
Jews supposed Paul a threat to the law and the Temple. In Rome
he had turned to the Gentiles, and the Jews saw no threat. In
Ephesus Paul had offended the businessmen, even before he had
offended the authorities.[10] In Rome Paul threatened no business interests. In Thessalonica (17:6) the charge of peace-breaking was
made, and Paul was forced to leave the city. In Rome Paul's move-

ments were restricted, and no official saw in him a threat to the peace of the city.

One of Luke's purposes in writing Acts may have been to show that the Christian faith was not a political movement. Individual Christians were not political agitators, but law-abiding citizens. These believers interpreted their faith in terms of absolute allegiance. Those most loyal to their Lord were, in most instances, most loyal to the state—because of their loyalty to their Lord. The principle extends to the present: "What is decisive is not the government's policy toward the Christian religion but the meaning of Jesus' lordship in relation to the political allegiance." [11]

In such a spirit of freedom, the book of Acts concludes. To be sure, Paul was a prisoner; but his bonds did not bind him from proclaiming the gospel. In a sense the reader forgets the bonds and celebrates the freedom of the good news. Acts does not conclude in these final verses, for the work goes on through the ministry of many. All involved are important. Unless all work together, the mission cannot be all God intends. The same Jesus is standing at the right hand of God, absent from believers in the flesh, yet present with them in the Spirit. The same Spirit, who moved upon the church at Pentecost, and directed its mission to all God's world, is acting today. The apostles have been replaced by modern witnesses, but the Spirit is the same. The Acts of the Apostles is not a closed book so long as God's Spirit moves God's people into God's world to be working together in Christ's mission.

5. Truth for Today

Apparent failure may disguise real success. God frequently molds our apparent failure into spiritual success. Although Paul was not able to bridge with his offering the gap in Jewish and Gentile relations, and although he was imprisoned in Caesarea and Rome, he did attain an unfettered gospel in Rome.

Uncontrolled prejudice is senseless and merciless. Men sometimes will go to any length to injure the object of their hate. Paul's mission to the Gentiles had made him unacceptable to many Jews. The latter had dogged his steps all over the world, determined to kill him.

God presides over human affairs. He even may use unlikely human allies to accomplish his purpose. The use of Cyrus in the Old Testament is paralleled in Acts by God's use of Roman military officers.

The gospel will not be accepted by all men. This is true despite the skill with which it is presented. The motif of rejection runs as clearly through the narrative as that of repentance and faith. A witness may give his life in faithful and capable teaching and/or preaching, but some people will reject God's revelation.

God's love both toughens and sensitizes. It emboldens the Christian witness in crises, but makes him tender to human need. Paul felt compassion for the father of Publius, even after the ordeal of the voyage and shipwreck.

The clearest Christian witness is simply, "It happened to me." Again and again Paul spoke of his own experience with the risen Christ. That kind of witness is clear and effective.

---

[1] Richard Lovelace, "To Althea from Prison," in *Familiar Quotations,* ed. by John Bartlett (Boston: Little, Brown and Company, 1955), p. 268.

[2] Josephus, *op. cit.,* p. 596.

[3] The question of Paul's financial resources is intriguing. He had many expenses in these final movements: the Temple vow for the four men, the trial, his self-support. He was treated with respect all along the way, and Felix even hoped to receive a bribe from him. Possible sources were limited. Was he being supported by gifts from the churches, or perhaps even by Luke's fees? Some suppose that Paul had received part of a family inheritance. There is no evidence that he worked with his hands during this period.

[4] Numbers 6:1-21 suggests some of the details. Paul himself had come to Jerusalem on a previous occasion (18:18) under a vow.

[5] Stagg, *op. cit.,* p. 223.

[6] Some Greek manuscripts add here a thinly veiled accusation against Claudius Lysias. The gist of that accusation made by Tertullus against Claudius was that the latter had interfered in a matter which belonged in Jewish hands. These verses do not appear, however, in the most reliable manuscripts.

[7] James Smith, *The Voyage and Shipwreck of St. Paul* (London: Longman, Brown, et al, 1856). This book offers many nautical details about the voyage.

[8] Paul clearly had turned to the Gentiles at other times, as indicated in 9:15, 13:46, and 18:6.

[9] Acts omits any mention of Paul's death. Tradition has offered various theories, including the suggestion that he was released from this first imprisonment at Rome for an extended ministry, only to be arrested again and executed. Luke was more concerned about Paul's standing with responsible Roman authorities than with his conviction at the hands of a less responsible authority (Nero?).

[10] Keck, *op. cit.,* p. 150: "Because the church is not a political party, its impact is not restricted to the realignment of the government, but affects the economy as well. In our society, which is dominated by business, we need to ponder the fact that in Acts it was the businessmen who were offended by the results of the gospel before the police were." Used by permission.

[11] *Ibid.,* p. 146.

Personal Learning Activities

Chapter 1

1. Identify with Theophilus and consider the "treatise" as addressed to yourself. In fifty words or less state the main theme of the book. (Hint: Is the Acts of the Apostles a good name for this book?)

2. What difference did the coming of the Holy Spirit make in the church at Jerusalem?

Chapter 2

1. How do the problems and their solutions as described in Chapter 2 throw light on difficulties in your own church?

2. What is the Holy Spirit leading you to do with respect to problem areas in your church?

Chapter 3

1. How does Stephen's apology speak to the modern church and the world beyond?

2. List the two nonapostolic men who acted heroically in Acts 6:8 to 8:40, naming at least one significant action of each one.

Chapter 4

1. How does the picture of Peter in Acts resemble that of the Gospels? How does it differ?

2. In Chapter 4 note the basic church problem that Peter faced and overcame, and relate how the Holy Spirit led the church through Peter's action.

Chapter 5

1. What does the expansion of Christianity from Jerusalem to Damascus, Antioch, and beyond mean to today's churches, especially with respect to their worldwide mission?

2. Discuss the merits of the Antioch church's decision to give its choice leadership to the world mission.

Chapter 6

1. What were the real issues at the Jerusalem Council?

2. What does the Jerusalem Council teach us about the Spirit's power to lead a church that is in conflict? What hinders the Spirit's leadership?

Chapter 7

1. Read Acts 16:6-10, looking for ways the Spirit led Paul and his party. Can you find any evidences of the Spirit's leading by ordinary means? If so, what? (See the section in Chapter 7 entitled "Finding God's Will.")

2. Read Paul's letter to Philippi (1:1-11; 2:19-30; 4:10-20) and the Acts account of Paul's ministry there (Acts 16:11-40). In what ways did the Philippians remain true friends of the apostle?

Chapter 8

1. Note several basic differences between Paul's ministry in small towns and his ministry in urban areas.

2. Could Paul have met the philosophers in Athens or the Jews in Corinth on more friendly terms and yet have been true to his gospel?

Chapter 9

1. How does the social setting in which a church functions pose a threat to Christ's mission?

2. What potential dangers to the church are implied in Paul's charge to the elders (20:18-35)? Are they similar to current dangers?

Chapter 10

1. Which was the greater threat to the Christian mission: Roman law or Jewish prejudice? Which is the greater threat today: law or prejudice? Why?

2. Review the three accounts of Paul's conversion (9:1-19, 22:3-21, 26:2-23), and note the unique features in each.

THE CHURCH STUDY COURSE

The Church Study Course provides a comprehensive series of courses organized into 18 subject areas dealing with knowledge, understanding, and skills needed for growth toward Christian maturity and competence in Christian service.

This book is the basic content for course 3215, *Acts: Working Together in Christ's Mission.* Credit is granted to adults and youth when application is made for class study, for individual study, or for reading the course materials.

In the Church Study Course, completion of prescribed courses leads to one of 14 diplomas. Detailed information about Church Study Course and the system of credits, diplomas, and record keeping may be obtained from the following Southern Baptist agencies or from the corresponding office in state Baptist conventions:

The Sunday School Board, 127 Ninth Avenue, North, Nashville, Tenn. 37234;

Woman's Missionary Union, 600 North 20th Street, Birmingham, Ala. 35203;

Brotherhood Commission, 1548 Poplar Avenue, Memphis, Tenn. 38104.

The following requirements must be met for 3 credits in course 3215:

1. Read the book *Acts: Working Together in Christ's Mission.*

2. Attend at least 7½ hours of class study or complete all "Personal Learning Activities" (pp. 139-140). Class members who are absent from one or more class sessions must complete "Personal Learning Activities" on chapters missed. In such a case, he must turn in his paper by the date the teacher sets, usually within ten days following the last class.

The following requirements must be met for 2 credits in course 3215:

1. Read the book.

2. Attend at least 5 hours of class study. Class members who miss one or more class sessions must complete "Personal Learning

Activities" on chapters missed. In such a case he must turn in his paper by the date the teacher sets, usually within ten days following the last class.

The following requirements must be met for 1 credit in course 3215:

1. Read the book.

Request for Course Credit, Form 151, or the individual request for credit form on page 144 should be completed and mailed to Church Study Course Awards Office, 127 Ninth Avenue, North, Nashville, Tennessee 37234. Credit should be requested for the teacher. The director of Church Training, or the person designated by the church, should complete and sign Form 151. Two copies of the course credit award will be sent by the Church Study Course Awards Office to the church. One copy should be filed in the Church Training record, and the other given to the individual.

Cut along this line

- -

INSTRUCTIONS: If requested by the teacher, fill in this form and give it to him when the course is completed. If preferred, mail this request for course credit to

AWARDS-MAILING LIST UNIT
RESEARCH SERVICES DEPARTMENT
THE SUNDAY SCHOOL BOARD, SBC
127 NINTH AVENUE, NORTH
NASHVILLE, TENNESSEE 37234

Indicate Type of Study (√)　　☐ Individual　　☐ Class　　☐ Reading

State Convention　　Association　　Church Name

Address of Church (Street, Route, or P.O. Box)　　City　　State　　Zip Code

Mail to: (If different from church address)　　Address (Street, Route, or P.O. Box)　　City　　State　　Zip Code

LAST NAME,　　FIRST NAME,　　MIDDLE　　MRS. (X)

COURSE TITLE	Course Code	Credit	Hours
Acts: Working Together in Christ's Mission	3215		